# Bexhill Voices Two

edited by

Aylwin Guilmant

Bexhill Voices Two

First published 1999

ISBN 0 9535257 0 8

Published by Bexhill Voices Two, Catavia, 18, Richmond Road, Bexhill-on-Sea, East Sussex TN39 3DN

Desktop published using Pressworks, typeset in Palatino

Printed by Barnes Watson Printing, 20, Windsor Road, Bexhill-on-Sea, East Sussex TN39 3BA

# CONTENTS

| | |
|---|---|
| Acknowledgements | iv |
| Preface | vi |
| Introduction | 1 |
| R.A. Larkin & Bros. Ltd. | 20 |
| Geoff Larkin The Human Torpedo | 24 |
| Phyllis Burl | 30 |
| Joan Bush née Warburton | 44 |
| Norman Cook | 49 |
| Peter Evenden | 72 |
| William Gordon Harris | 85 |
| Mollie Hickie née Willing | 94 |
| Ted Hollands | 107 |
| Pauline Lane née Cook | 121 |
| Peter Longley | 126 |
| George Ransom | 135 |
| Ernest Claude Solomon | 144 |

# Acknowledgements

Rother District Council.

Bexhill Museum.

The *Daily Mail* for article and photographs in connection with Geoff Larkin.

John Dowling and the *Bexhill Observer* for additional material in connection with R. A. Larkin Bros. Ltd. and Geoff Larkin.

We are grateful to the following for the use of their photographs —
- Ted Mepham
- David Warburton
- Mrs. M. Wharton

Our particular thanks go to Alan Beecher for the time-consuming work undertaken in connection with the computer typesetting, page layout and editorial assistance for Bexhill Voices Two.

We are very grateful to the following benefactors, both individual and organisations, for their much appreciated contributions without which this book would never have been published.

Messrs. Geoff and Jack Larkin

Mr. Norman Cook

Mr. W. Gordon Harris

Mr. Humphry Smith O.B.E.

The Old Town Preservation Society

The Association of Bexhill Citizens

Messrs. Gaby Hardwicke Yearwood & Griffiths (Solicitors)

Messrs. Rush, Witt & Wilson (Estate Agents)

# PREFACE

The original group as named in *Bexhill Voices* worked very hard to obtain a selection of tapes from as wide a number of interviewees as possible and many were disappointed to find that only 14 of the original number were included in that book.

It is with this in mind that a small group of like-minded people have come together to produce this sequel consisting of the unused original interviews plus additional material.

The first team met on a regular basis once a week, originally at the Museum but after a short while in a private house; they were a very dedicated group, sadly today depleted by death. They were also fortunate to have the services of Dr. Fred Gray of the Centre of Continuing Education and the financial backing of the University of Sussex.

Today we are without this support. Not only have the following persons, Alan Beecher, Aylwin Guilmant, Brenda Mason, Jill Theis and Margaret Woolf, given their time freely but they have also been considerably involved in fund-raising in order for this project to be completed within a reasonable time-scale. Without the financial support of our benefactors (listed on a separate page) none of this would have been possible. We are most grateful for the financial help we have received from organisations and professional bodies but also individuals for their donations towards the cost of getting *Bexhill Voices Two* into print.

We feel strongly that a book of this nature is part of our Town's history and it is with this in mind that we have undertaken this work. We hope that future generations will see their way forward to continuing this local historical project into the next millenium.

# INTRODUCTION

This book does not set out to be a history of Bexhill rather it is the story of certain individuals who grew up in the town earlier this century. It concentrates mainly on their formative years but in some instances education continued into their later lives, therefore this has been included.

The war was a catalyst for many of those interviewed, people who were involved in it rarely speak of the impact it would have made on them. However, their happier early years must have sustained them because as adults they returned to either work here, or, with one exception, to retire here.

The ghost town of the years of the Second World War with its diminished population and high military presence disappeared almost overnight with the commencement of the Second Front. Having suffered through the vicissitudes of war, loss of life and buildings to bombs and 'doodle-bugs', the town gradually recovered with the return of its active young men and women.

The Council policy of the post-war years saw many of the old landmarks disappear in the name of progress, among them the wooden buildings linking the town with the King's German Legion stationed here during the Napoleonic Wars.

Bexhill is still in an expanding situation, the population has risen from 12,000 at the turn of the century to an estimated figure of over 40,000 today. Rother District Council working closely with other organisations is intent on improving the quality of life for the inhabitants, the 'Spirit of Place' programme, of which the first stage has already commenced. Bexhill, still continues to attract large numbers of tourists from both home and abroad

## The De La Warr influence in Bexhill-on-Sea.

The most important factor in the rise of modern Bexhill was the coming of the railway in 1846 when the London Brighton and South Coast company opened its single line between Lewes and Bulverhythe. Much of the land through which it ran was owned by the De La Warr Estate and the 5th Earl stipulated that Bexhill should have a railway halt to serve the small village on the hill, now the Old Town.

Bexhill-on-Sea was the last of the seaside towns to be built mainly through the involvement of an aristocratic family. The 7th Earl De La Warr had been responsible for a sea wall on the eastern side of the town. He also promoted the local gas and water companies and taking a lesson from the Duke of Devonshire at the nearby town of Eastbourne started a programme of residential building. It was he who also added the words on-Sea' to its name in 1884, thereby announcing its intention of joining the seaside resort race.

His second son, Gilbert George Reginald Viscount Cantelupe (1869-1915) became his father's heir and subsequently 8th Earl. He married Muriel Brassey and lived at the Manor House. During the years of his first marriage the Earl had close links with the town, he was involved in local government and became chairman of the town's first Urban Council on the death of Colonel Henry Lane in 1895. The Earl was involved in instigating the first speed trials along East and De La Warr Parades. He was also responsible for the building of the Kursaal entertainment hall, in bringing members of the aristocracy to his house in the Old Town and engaging in advertising and promoting Bexhill as a residential town and seaside resort; it is believed that he spent much of his personal wealth in so doing.

It was the 8th Earl who strove hard to obtain a Charter of Incorporation for the town and Bexhill became the last Sussex town to achieve this in 1902. Despite his many interests and diligence in promoting the town the Earl was overlooked as a candidate for the mayoralty of the new Borough due to his divorce and a smear campaign mounted against him. However, he became Mayor in 1903.

The 8th Earl was also responsible for the formation of the famous Cooden Beach golf course. This was laid out by the Earl over the old Cooden Manor estate and opened in 1912. According to Earnest Claude Solomon, born in a railway cottage at Cooden, 'I used to go out and earn about half a crown, I used to go up there before I left school and remember the girls caddying. They used to wear rompers and lace-up

The Manor House in Old Town was bought by Bexhill Corporation in 1965 for £23,000 and ultimately demolished it a year or so later. From 1892 the 8th Earl and his bride lived there until their divorce. The house was used by the young couple for lavish entertainments for distinguished visitors including royalty.

Celebration of 25th anniversary of Charter Day, Bexhill-on-Sea. 20th July 1927.

boots.' Ted Hollands recalls the many people who 'would come down (from London) and go back again in a day.' Apparently just to play golf.

When the Earl died on active service at the relatively early age of 46 in 1915, he was mourned as ' the maker of modern Bexhill.'

In 1933 the 9th Earl De La Warr was elected Mayor of Bexhill, a post which he held until 1935. He was a socialist and he had sided with Ramsay MacDonald after the divisions in the Labour Party in 1931.

The Earl was eager to promote the town and it was at his instigation that an architectural competition for the Bexhill Pavilion was organised. At this time it was felt that Bexhill was losing potential holiday makers because it had no modern entertainment hall. Despite some opposition to the scheme the De La Warr Pavilion was opened in 1935. Peter Evenden, a youth of 15 remembered that his parents were in favour, 'there was a lot of discussion but I think most everybody felt that an entertainment hall as it was called would be a great addition...'

The De La Warr Pavilion, erected as a people's palace by the sea, became one of Europe's most important interwar structures, being the first major welded steel frame building in England and was pioneering in construction, form and spirit.

Childrens' boating pool, Pavilion, Colonnade and West Parade, Bexhill-on-Sea.

The Opening Ceremony by the Duke and Duchess of York, in December 1935, created a stir in the community; one child from every school was invited to attend, while others lined the route waving their Union Jacks in welcome to their Royal visitors.

The current restoration programme will develop the Pavilion into a Centre for the Visual Arts and Architecture as well as a regional theatre and recreational venue by the sea (few other entertainment and leisure buildings can claim such a perfect site).

In its early years the De La Warr Pavilion was used by young and old alike. Deck games were enjoyed by many people who found the flat roof reminiscent of an ocean liner. This scheme was echoed by the older visitors who lined the balconies with their deck chairs, soaking up the sun. The Pavilion was built for the people of Bexhill and it is hoped that the present and future generations will take advantage of the increase in space for use by community groups. Today the De La Warr Pavilion is known world wide and evokes much interest among visitors from home and abroad. The present Earl takes an active interest in the restoration programme to a building carrying his name.

The names of the De La Warr family are also perpetuated in many of the streets of Bexhill, for instance Cantelupe, Lionel, Richmond and others to be found in the book of *Bexhill Street Names* (Bexhill Museum Association, 1996).

Bexhill Borough ceased to exist in 1974 and Rother District Council came into being. Many of the older Bexhillians mourn this loss. 'The Mayor was held in very high esteem in those days and to me at least it was a tragedy and I don't think it has been good for Bexhill. The De La Warr family had influence but were not dominant'. So claims one of those interviewed, who felt that with the passing of the Council, Bexhill had lost much of her identity. However Rother District Council are today fostering a new spirit of optimism in the various aspects of the town under review.

## The Growth of the new Town

During the first fifty years of this century the town of Bexhill remained little changed, despite the havoc caused by bombing raids and later the flying bomb, (known as doodle bugs'). Phyllis Burl remembered her former employer, 'He wanted me to go away because he didn't want me to be on my own in the shop. So I went to my auntie in Wales and when I was there the shop was blown up and poor Mr Collis was killed.'

Central Parade and War Memorial, Bexhill-on-Sea.

Bexhill was a town of late Victorian and Edwardian buildings, large seaside hotels, purpose built independent boarding schools and small family run shops. The parents of the pupils of these schools came first to the town as visitors and on their retirement from posts abroad settled here. Mollie Hickie was a pupil at one of these schools because her father 'was an employee of the Bank of British West Africa.' Longleys store first developed through the fact that 'they were making-up clothes for the wives and daughters of the considerable number of retired colonial and service people who were coming to live in the town' and, 'A bill-head for 1913 advertised that the shop would provide "Indian and Colonial Outfits" and mourning attire for both "family" and "complementary" wear.'

During both World Wars Bexhill was in the front-line. South African and Canadian troops were stationed here in the Great War while in

World War 2 British and Canadian soldiers and the RAF occupied many of the large buildings. The inhabitants not engaged on essential war work were encouraged to evacuate and the population was reputed to be as low as 5,000 in the latter months of 1940, it was certainly possible to walk down Devonshire Road and not meet a living soul. Pauline Lane and her family 'evacuated ourselves to Cambridge but not for long. We came back to a house partly damaged by bombs. I remember sitting sunbathing in the garden at the time of Dunkirk and seeing a great black cloud of smoke covering the sky drifting down Channel. There was barbed wire on the beaches and the town was eerily empty for long periods'.

Bomb damage in Station Road may have been due to the 'tip and run' raids of 1942

In 1939 Bexhill had been a reception area for London children and the state school buildings were shared with local children only having a part-time education, however following the fall of the Low Countries in 1940 there was large-scale civilian evacuation with children from state schools going to Bedfordshire and Hertfordshire. Other independent schools had to make their own arrangements. Messrs. Sargents and T. Mepham & Sons were the two firms most involved in this operation. According to Ted Mepham, 'many of the town's residents chose to leave for safer areas as well and there was considerable demand for storage'. Thornbank School was one of the buildings so used. During World War I we read in *Bexhill Voices* of the tradesmen having their horses requisitioned, while in World War II Mepham's newest vehicle was requisitioned for war service, never to be seen again. This firm also lost some of their premises through enemy bombing and as a consequence they purchased the old St. Barnabas School in Western Road (at one time Phyllis Burl had been a pupil there) now the Library and 'quickly filled it with the furniture from many households'.

Van 13 from left to right Alec Sinclair, Vic Spray and Charlie Waters. In 1939 a tow bar was fitted for towing a pump and it served two nights each weekas a fire engine when it was driven by E. G. Mepham on those occasions. During 1940 the van was used to help with the evacuation of Bexhill schools.

The evacuation of the private schools became the death knell of many, those that survived and returned to the town continued to operate, some with fewer pupils than pre 1939 but during the 1960s and later their large playing fields and surroundings came to be seen as valuable building land by the many speculators in this business. The schools 'sold-out', some at such short notice that children with parents abroad were faced with the threat of having no boarding place, this naturally created much panic fortunately those still remaining in operation were able to take in the displaced pupils. Out of a pre-war figure of between thirty and forty schools only three independent ones remain. Few of the original purpose built structures exist; Loreto Convent is now Hollenden House, a home for ex-servicemen and women; Collington Rise School and Lake House are both now made into flats. St. Mary's School for disabled children is sited at the former Lindores School. This building was originally the home of Sir Edward and Lady Ermyntrude Malet; the name is preserved in the Malet Hall erected by Lady Ermyntrude, a cousin of the 8th Earl De La Warr, in memory of her husband.

Peter Longley recalls, 'At the age of eight I went to Collington Rise School. The building is now flats at the bottom end of Collington Rise, and the school chapel, which was built while I was at school, is in what is now Birkdale, though at that time it was part of the school playing fields.'

The private schools have played a large part in the development of the town, they created work, both directly and indirectly. Some of the mothers of those interviewed first arrived in Bexhill as domestics employed in the schools. Norman Cook's mother came from Gloucester and 'started as a parlour-maid in the Beehive School at the bottom of Dorset Road.' George Ransom's mother 'took in washing from a Collington Lane school (Effingham House) and that was delivered by the local pigman, G.S. Allen. Nice big basket of washing, 150 girls. I remember rows of washing.' Other schools patronised the many laundries which catered for their needs together with the large hotels and boarding houses.

The schools created employment within the town, they were served by the local shops. Mr Minor, who set-up William Gordon Harris' mother in a shop of this name, 'rode around the town on a large heavy bike taking samples of shoes to the independent boarding schools in the area; the Matrons being responsible for ordering a selection of shoes as required by the pupils.' It must be remembered that at this time many of the pupils had parents overseas. Phyllis Burl worked as a trainee book-keeper at Collis the chemist. 'I remember we had 900 accounts, so there was quite a lot to do. Some schools used to have not only the personal accounts of the children but they also had photography accounts as well.'

Parents who visited their children while on leave stayed at the many hotels and on retiring from overseas settled here. These people, often with money and influence, grasped the opportunity to serve the town, particularly during the period from 1890-1945. However they were not always popular with the residents, Ernest Claude Solomon remembered the snobbery amongst some of the wealthier Cooden residents. He hated 'people coming up to me and saying "Good afternoon Solomon." That gets up my goat. I can't stick it.' However he felt that the war brought people together.

Pre 1939 both Sidley and Little Common were quite separate from the rest of the town. Norman Cook remembers where Buxton Drive is now built 'there were just two large green gates there, with fields beyond where you were able to get to London Road, which at that time ceased in the vicinity of Cambridge Road.' It was certainly possible to walk across fields from Sidley to Little Common before the building of the Whitehouse Farm and Glenleigh Park estates. While from the Old Town it was possible to travel much of the way through farmland to Sidley. Norman Cook saw his 'life in the village as a simple life in a closely knit community.' George Ransom born there in 1917 called himself a 'Sidleyite.' The people who lived in these areas thought of themselves as separate from the rest of the town, they had their own places of amusement though some of the older teenagers preferred the greater excitement of Bexhill to that of the villages. 'We used to go to Bexhill a lot 'cause there was a fun fair along the front by the old pavilion, not the De La Warr.' Life for children of the interwar years was simple, they had few expectations and these were usually met in their own environment. Some of those interviewed remembered playing in the streets with hoops and other inexpensive toys, or games such as 'grandmother's footsteps, skatums and conkers. I once had a "44er" which meant that my conker had defeated that many others.'

There were certain favourite areas, Collington Woods was one, the Hollow (now the site of the 'West Indies' blocks of flats on West Parade) another. However at one time it had been used as a miniature golf course, with clock golf being played on an open grassy plot opposite the Arundel Hotel in Park Avenue.

Sidley High Street early this century. On the right may be seen the Beal Catt forge and adjoining cottage.

Little Common c. 1912 showing the crossroads with the distinctive grassy areas now the site of the roundabout.

Organised games were played in the park by children from the many small town centre private schools, other children had drill with dumbbells and Indian clubs on the area between the two rows of coastguard cottages (now the site of the De La Warr Pavilion) or played wild games of hide-and-seek in the shrubs above the Colonnade.

The Promenade and beach were the playground of local child and visitor alike. There are many who remember staying with a relative or in one of the many seaside hotels who were never at a loss for amusement. Sand castle competitions were organised on the beach. There were two popular Bathing Stations, Buxton's and Howes. They had small changing cabins and from these to the water's edge ran coconut matting which always smelt of the sea. Offshore there were rafts anchored and it was a challenge to swim out and dive off them. The children of parents who owned their own beach-huts were always faintly envious of these amenities as they had to make-do with the few large breakwaters which dotted the foreshore. One of the most popular was opposite the flagstaff at the end of West Parade. Along the beach from here stretched the remains of the promenade extension built in 1912 and destroyed in a gale that same year. The cliffs at South Cliff were a challenge to the young as they were still unspoilt. All the private schools offered swimming in their prospectuses, not many of the schools had their own pool but went to either a hut on the beach or to the Egerton Park pool. Certain of the families enjoyed the amenities. Both Peter Longley and Peter Evenden went swimming on a regular basis with their fathers. Sandown Preparatory School (together with many others) were justly proud of their claim that every child could swim before they left there, despite not having a school pool.

Few of those interviewed went on holiday, or if they did, they went to relatives. 'I didn't go away much but I used to stay with my grannie, my dad's mother, at Ringmer. They had a farm and I used to wear the old fashioned plimsolls, my feet got soft walking up through the stubble, that's where I went for my summer holidays.' However, people did take picnics, either to the beach or the countryside. Mollie Hickie a pupil at St. John's School 'enjoyed picnics in Collington Woods. We were each given a "nose-bag", a white paper bag containing a hard-

Buxton's Bathing Station, West Parade, Bexhill-on-Sea.

Bexhill-on-Sea. The Parade.

boiled egg, some lettuce leaves, a meat pie, a bun and an apple or banana.' While Pauline Lane felt no need for a holiday. 'If we did go away we might go to the country to stay at a farm or guest houses. Sometimes we might have a day out, perhaps go to a tea garden.'

Tea gardens were very popular during the inter-war years, also small cafes serving coffee and cream teas. Bexhill had a number of these and during the war they were well patronised because eating in one saved one's rations. One of the biggest and most popular was Arscott's in St. Leonards Road.

Most of Bexhill's expanding population pre 1939 lived in modern houses, many of them built post the 1914-18 war. The wealthier element, of which there was a considerable number of well connected people, lived in large detached houses in West Bexhill and Cooden; however certain of the roads were still unmade. There were few flats, Brookfield and Motcombe Court had been built and the earlier block Marina Court (now demolished) 'used to be a colossal building, Findlaters on the corner facing east used to be a big wine merchant. There was another shop there sold materials.' This building, together with the Metropole Hotel, Roberts Marine Mansions and Glyne Hall (at the bottom of Sea Road) were the core of early Edwardian buildings in the centre of the town.

Devonshire Road was an important shopping centre with Longleys Department Store at the southern end. It was rare for shops to remain empty for very long, even during the worst years of the Depression and during wartime. Today many of these premises are occupied by Building Societies and Estate Agents. Previously there had been shops selling a variety of goods from pianos to 'best butter at 1/9d. per pound.' Phyllis Burl remembered that 'There was a big toy shop called the Devonshire Emporium. No-one seems to remember it but me. It was a big toy shop and it sold big toys like motor cars and tricycles and things that cost a lot of money.' In this thoroughfare it was possible to buy just about everything, fruit, meat, fish, vegetables, groceries, sweets, furniture, hardware, pharmaceutical products, shoes and clothes for all the family and with the coming of Woolworth, everything for 6d. St. Leonards Road also was a popular shopping area, particularly during

Devonshire Road, Bexhill-on-Sea.

the time of Millers and Franklin's store which occupied three corner sites. It employed nearly a hundred people, as did Longley Bros. Another large store, Green's, was in Sackville Road. These shops offered employment to both men and women. Western Road had a cinema, garage, Timothy White's and Hodgkinson's furniture shop. It was always considered a cheaper shopping area. Today it has a thriving network of shops offering a variety of goods. Most of the town centre was tree lined, including Sea Road, and people enjoyed shopping in such pleasant surroundings

Some of the men interviewed had first started their working life as errand boys. George Ransom mentioned that 'I remember all the errand boys of Sidley. We would chase down to the beach with your old-fashioned costume at 10 o'clock at night after work. Leave our bikes, they wouldn't get pinched.' Despite long hours people did not complain, they took pride in their work and were prepared to give of their best. Ted Hollands felt that 'Bexhill has not improved. Its gone down terrible. Well, I can remember the road sweepers, for instance, all had their own allotted span of roads to keep clean.' Today much of this work is carried out by machines. People also took a pride in the appearance of their houses and the pavement outside. Bexhill was in a very pleasant situation, there was open countryside close by, green areas within the town centre, country lanes and the many playing fields surrounding the private schools.

People remembered the part that the church played in their lives, while their parents may not have been regular churchgoers children were sent to Sunday School. Those who attended church always wore their best clothes. The Gordon Harris girls were dressed alike in 'navy blue princess line dresses with red leather belts, white collars with a red bow, woollen stockings and red "Charleston" sandals. After church we always went for a walk on the sea front.' Pauline Lane always dressed in her 'Sunday best' with 'patent leather shoes', the hats were velour in winter and usually panama in summer. The children at the boarding schools had special Sunday wear. Mollie Hickie recalls wearing 'white elbow length gloves'. Often the schools were the larger part of the church congregation. Following church many of them went on 'their advertisement walks' along the sea front.

Bexhill Swimming Club Float at an early Bexhill Carnival on West Parade.

Children were encouraged to attend Sunday School by the attraction of a special Sunday School outing. Phyllis Burl remembers going as far afield as Goudhurst. Others 'were sort of made to go to church' both in the morning and the afternoon.

Certain events stand out in the lives of those interviewed. The carnivals and pageants, especially those for the Jubilee and Coronation celebrations. 'Mother built up a reputation as depicting Britannia. Her costume was made of white muslin, her shield made from a wooden hoop belonging to Ivy Furner and covered with a Union Jack. The helmet was made from a fireman's helmet belonging to the local Fire Chief, Mr Bodle, which was painted with gold paint and a plume attached. We always made our own costumes from bits and pieces.'

An occasion of a different nature was that which took place at the War Memorial at 11 a.m. on the 11th November every year. Children from many of the local schools attended and were made aware of the solemnity of the service and what it represented. William Gordon Harris tells of his sister, Bunty, a Guide, carrying their banner. The two-minute silence made a deep impact on the young.

A happy interlude in the lives of those interviewed was Sir Alan Cobham's air circus which visited Little Common in 1933. One of those interviewed was fortunate to go up for a short 5/- flight. While those others had to make do with any vantage point from which to watch the aerial event, little knowing that within a very short time they would be watching the Battle of Britain in the skies overhead.

While the children growing up between the wars did not suffer the hardships experienced by those whose stories are told in *Bexhill Voices* nevertheless life was considerably harder than it is today. They were prepared to earn pennies for the cinema or to help out generally with the family finances. Food was sometimes in short supply, fathers were stood-off from work, particularly during bad weather, mothers were forced to take-in washing in order to survive and children collected manure (which was deposited in the street) and sold it for 1d. a bucket.

Children thought nothing of walking alone quite long distances to school at an early age. 'I still wonder how we ever got to school, as the eldest of us was only seven years of age. Didn't have anyone to look after us with all our crowd but we never got into too much trouble.'

Boys experienced the cane for misbehaviour, but none felt that they had been victimised, however Ernest Claude Solomon felt he should not have been punished for something he did after school, but his headmaster felt otherwise!

Those interviewed felt that their life in Bexhill had been a happy one and they were content to return here on their retirement.

The population of the town is rising with many young families moving into the area, shops in the town centre are reopening and the first stage of Bexhill High School has been completed on the new site in Gunters Lane. First year pupils have started there.

Bexhill Regeneration Partnership Ltd., with Rother District Council have been successful in attracting investment back into the town and have made a bid for funds in order to generate help for some disadvantaged areas.

The restoration of the De La Warr Pavilion is proceeding. The 'Spirit of Place' initiative in Western Road has been completed and further work within the town is under consideration.

The Old Town Preservation Society is working hard to improve the Old Town and is also closely involved with other projects. The lighting in the Manor Gardens has now been completed.

The Association of Bexhill Citizens is actively involved in replacing many of the town's trees, a feature of the past and sadly missed today.

Jarvis Cooden Beach Hotel, Bexhill 100 and Bexhill Museum have put on a display of photographs relating to the history of the early motor racing in the town at the Cooden Beach Hotel.

The new voice of the Chamber of Commerce is being heard.

The Town Forum is working closely with Rother District Council on many projects. The voice of the children has been heard, a cycle track is contemplated and a skateboard and roller blade site has been constructed.

Bexhill is fortunate to have two Museums on two separate sites. The Bexhill Museum has embarked on a programme especially aimed at attracting the young to their site with workshops, walks and other activities designed to appeal to them. While the Bexhill Museum of Costume and Social History is a popular venue for groups with specialised interests.

Finally, Bexhill Tourist Information Centre reported an upsurge of visitors from home and abroad during 1997.

Footnote: *Aylwin Guilmant comes from an old Sussex family; her grandparents came to Bexhill early in the 20th century. She was born in the town and most of her life has been spent here. She married an architect and raised four daughters. She has eight grandchildren and great-grandchildren. She is a past chairman of the governers of Bexhill High School and was a member of the Samaritans organisation for 28 years from 1964. One of the first graduates of the Open University she has been awarded a M. Phil. degree by the University of Kent for a thesis on the 19th century Earls of Ashburnham and their Sussex Estate. Subsequently she became a part-time tutor for the CCE University of Sussex. She has had 12 books published by Phillimore and Sutton Publishing and the County series of 'One Hundred Years Ago' has been reprinted and distributed world-wide. Her interests are her family and friends. She is a local speaker on various topics and enjoys tennis.*

# R.A. LARKIN & BROS. LTD.

One of the best known firms to operate for over sixty years (1924 - 1988) was that of R.A. Larkin & Bros. Ltd. and throughout these years the name became synonymous with quality, to such an extent that even today, ten years after the company sold out to Prowtings Southern, estate agents still advertise many of their sales as 'a Larkin built property', often as a guarantee of a ready sale.

When Reg Larkin first came to Bexhill he started sub-contracting in Knebworth Road. The conditions were shocking; Knebworth Road was knee-deep in mud. There was no road, only clay and the lorries were churning it up. Different builders were at work there and it was this fact that decided Reg to build houses that were complementary to one another.

Reg with his brother Jack built the first dwelling in Plemont Gardens. They built a hut in the grounds and used this as living accommodation while the work was in progress; they carried out this tradition of living on the premises for a number of years. The Larkin brothers went on to develop the north side of Cooden Drive from the brow of the hill (Pages Avenue) to opposite Beaulieu Road. Certain sceptics predicted that the development so close to the railway line would be a failure but time proved them wrong.

In 1933 Reg moved into 'Woodsgate Place' which had some 18 acres of grounds, which he proceeded to develop. This house became both his home and office, for by this time the firm were building over 100 houses a year.

When the White House Farm Estate was developed the firm took the old farm buildings, including the barn, as its workshops. At Newlands Avenue and White House Farm the firm built not only the homes but, for the first time undertook the construction of roads and sewers as well.

One event which influenced Reg Larkin when he first came to Bexhill in that early post-first world war period was the fact that as a plumber by trade he had been out of work for three months and realised that during inclement weather men in the building industry were suffering great hardship, being stood off for many months at a time. Therefore when he became an employer he decided to keep a small staff going all the year round by retaining some land for building spec' (speculative) houses while waiting for another contract to materialise. Latterly 85% of the work of this firm was building to contract on land which the company owned.

An early development was Walton Park. Individual houses were built in Cooden at Maple Walk and Clavering Walk, while at South Cliff, still an unmade road, 'the jewel in the crown' was 'Cordova' built for Sir Eustace Watkins, still amongst the most attractive of the houses in Bexhill. While on a more local note a large part of Broadoak Lane, Broad View and Ward Way were built on the site of Careys old brick yard.

The early years of the 30s were momentous ones for the company as the youngest brother, Geoff, joined the family firm, shortly followed by Norman Ward who held the post of Company Secretary until his death in 1982.

The Larkin brothers worked closely together until the outbreak of World War II, when Geoff, as a member of the RNVR went to serve his country. During this period the firm undertook what was known as 'term contract work' which meant that they looked after billets and military works. They built gun houses and pill boxes and serviced billets and private houses for about a ten-mile radius.

Following Geoff's return 'R.A. Larkin and Brothers Ltd.' became a private company in 1954, with Geoff doing the outside work, Jack the buying and heating calculations and Reg the forward planning. Subsequently Jack's son, John Larkin, became a director, his father sadly having died the same year as Norman Ward. The company continued to grow and employed around 150 men as direct employees. Very little sub-contract labour was used. Miss Margery Freeman was also a long term employee.

The post-war period saw a need for accommodation and certain old properties were converted into flats, including 'Millfield', a large Georgian mansion in Belle Hill. Other flats were built including the ones in the grounds of Normandale and Thornbank schools, and on the site of 'The Croft' and 'Stokes House', while the 'West Indies' blocks were erected over a period of time in the 60s with 174 flats in this complex alone.

Over the years the bulk of the dwellings have been bought by people who have retired, or are nearing retirement, which has led to criticism in some circles with the talk of an age imbalance, but an imbalance may have arisen through a variety of causes perhaps the most significant of these being the loss of a direct rail-link to the City and the closure of the many independent schools in the area.

Despite certain criticism Larkin built property is still as much in demand to-day as it was when it was first erected. In all, this Company planned, made-up and named 62 roads in addition to a further seven upon which they partially worked together with the buildings listed below:

| | |
|---|---|
| Church Extensions | 2 |
| Mortuaries | 2 |
| Sports Pavilions | 2 |
| Golf Clubhouse | 1 |
| Shops | 9 |
| Purpose-built Flats | 474 |
| Converted Flats | 169 |
| Houses & Bungalows | 2050 |
| Small Extensions Sunrooms etc. | 100 |
| total | 2889 |

Footnote: *Reg Larkin died in 1985 but the name lives on.*

Golden Anniversary of the founding of R.A.Larkin & Ltd. (1974). From left to right R.A.Larkin, Jack Larkin, Geoff Larkin and Norman Ward.

# G.J.W. Larkin — Human Torpedo

In 1942 in response to a Naval Signal, I volunteered for Special and hazardous service, and as a result was sent to Portsmouth for assessment. A diving course followed and in time I was sent to Scotland to join HMS Titania. Out of 100 volunteers, 30 completed this ardous training course in the near freezing waters of Loch Cairnbawn protected only by crude diving suits. After the initial training in oxygen breathing diving gear the new machine, a Two Man Torpedo arrived. The Unit was the 12th Submarine Flotilla.

The British craft was a hasty adaption of a concept pioneered with devastating results by the Italian Navy in the Mediterranean.

In an era before guided missiles the idea was to sit two men in crude 'frogman' kit astride a torpedo-like underwatercraft, driven by electric batteries. The total range of machine and diving gear was 18 miles and speed was 3 knots. The duration of the diving gear was 6 hours. Attacks were designed to take place in the dark. The breathing gear was rebreathing' and thus left no trail of bubbles.

The method of delivery in the Mediterranean was by a submarine, the Human Torpedo being carried in containers in the submarine's casing. My third mission was in January 1943 with an attack on Tripoli harbour.

The attack drill was to approach the target and position the removable warhead under the target vessel, detach the warhead of 400lbs., set a time clock and retire from the scene of operations. The clock was set for an agreed time to ensure that attackers did not interfere with each other. Each operation had a built-in escape plan. On the Tripoli attack the method was to land after the attack in North Africa and walk towards and endeavour to join up with the approaching 8th Army.

I was the driver and sitting behind was Len Berey, it was his responsibility to fix the warhead under the target. Due to mechanical problems with the machine we found ourselves stranded behind enemy lines and were captured by the German SS while hiding during daylight hours in a laager. After 14 hours as captives we managed to escape from the lorry in which we were imprisoned. We survived off the land eating lemon skins and drinking thick green water for two weeks before meeting up with a detachment of British troops.

I was also involved in attacks on Caglieri, then engaged in operations mounted from Lunna Voe in Scotland. The machines were transported by Motor Torpedo Boats (M.T.B's.), one on each quarter, and slung on davits. The M.T.B.'s landed an observer who kept in radio contact with and advised the M.T.B.'s of targets using the inner leads (which is the passage of water between the mainland and the islands) when they anchored.

Operations were mounted against the Tirpitz in Norwegian waters. Also in the Far East, and other targets in the Mediterranean.

By 1944, there was no further use for members of the 12th Flotilla and most of us were transferred, in one form or another, to the 182nd Minesweeping Flotilla, and, as divers, carried out mine disposal duties until the end of 1945.

Footnote: *Geoff, a very modest man, is one of Bexhill's local war heroes, as this method of warfare was unique in the annals of British Naval history. Recently Geoff has been thrilled to be presented with a model replica torpedo by Robert Hobson, who has just completed the first detailed historical book on the human torpedo.*

Geoff Larkin as he looked in W.W. II when he piloted the Human Torpedos.
(Photograph and caption by courtesy of the *Daily Mail*.)

# HEROES WHO SAT ASTRIDE TONS OF EXPLOSIVES UNDERWATER

## The human torpedoes

The human torpedo survivors' club reunion was a small, select affair.

Not surprising really, for what was held to be the most dangerous job in the Royal Navy in the Second World War.

Yesterday two elderly members of that distinguished group sat astride a restored version of one of their astonishing craft which would have been released from submarines to attack enemy battleships.

The intrepid crew, wearing primitive frogmen suits, would have steered the missile under the target's hull.

Then the nose of the torpedo containing the explosive charge was released and attached limpet-style to the ship. The men then had to beat a retreat in their battery-powered craft.

Originally the crewmen sat astride the Mark I torpedo as it was released, but in the Mark II version they crouched inside. Naval historian Robert Hobson discovered the rusting remains of this remarkable weapon in a Portsmouth dockyard and the Teesside Training and Enterprise Council near Middlesbrough took on the task of renovating it.

Mr Hobson first became aware of the story of the human torpedoes when clearing out his late father's house. Lieutenant Commander Robert Hobson had helped develop the human torpedoes and took part in several missions.

Mr Hobson, 56, said: 'I am a little sad that I never got to speak with my father about his missions but that was the way of these men, they never spoke of their bravery.'

Through his father's personal papers Mr Hobson tracked down two other torpedo pilots, Lieutenant Commander Geoff Larkin and Petty Officer Len Berey.

Human Torpedos piloted by W.W. II veterans Geoff Larkin (front) and Len Berey who straddled a Mark 1 again in front of the 'new' and larger Mark 2 in Teeside. (Photograph and caption by courtesy of the Daily Mail.)

'They asked for volunteers for special and hazardous missions,' said Mr Larkin. 'I was in America at the time and volunteered principally so I could return to England and get married.

I soon realised why they had the saying "never volunteer for anything".'

Mr Larkin, now 79, carried out two missions on the torpedoes, accompanied both times by Petty Officer Berey, now 83.

'It is great to see one of these back in business, it is right that their place in history is recorded,' said Mr Berey who comes from Northampton.

The torpedoes helped destroy 250,000 tons of enemy shipping. They gained vital intelligence on enemy positions and were used to deliver spies behind enemy lines.

On bombing missions the men would be kitted out in old fashioned diving suits with screw on helmets and gas masks. The primitive oxygen breathing cylinders had to be self contained to eliminate tell-tale bubbles rising to the surface. 'The men who carried out these missions were a special breed who put their lives on the line for King and country,' said Mr Hobson. 'They never spoke of their bravery and even today the Navy is reluctant to provide details. Advanced models of the human torpedoes are still used around the world today.'

Reprinted from the *Daily Mail,* August 20, 1997 by kind permission of the *Daily Mail.*

# Phylis Burl born 1914

I was born in 1914 in the coastguard cottages where the De La Warr Pavilion is now. I had one sister who was 8 years older than I was. I had a brother but he died. He was older than I was. He was born in 1910 and he died when he was a baby.

My father was a Prudential Insurance agent. Of course in the war nobody was taking out new insurances because the men were all away and it was all they could do to keep up the one's they had, so my father got very little money, and my mother took a job as the caretaker of the Sackville Road Methodist Church, which was only down Linden Road not very far away. She gave it up after the war. My father was a volunteer in the war. When he got his call-up papers he went for his medical and they classed him as C3 so they couldn't accept him. He didn't actually go to war.

Our house was nice because it was so near the sea. You could play on the lawn at the top, or just run down the slope to the sea. We often went bathing late at night or very early in the morning. And of course we had a lot of visitors because we were so near the sea and they liked that. The front room looked over the memorial to the Maharajah of Cooch Behar. There was one wash-house for each row of coastguard cottages. The boilers and taps were not in the house at all. Mother cooked on a range. We had beautiful brass lamps with coloured shades. And candles for upstairs. In 1919 gas lighting was laid on. I shared a room with my sister. I don't remember the rent on the coastguard cottage. (I remember the rent when we came here to 5, St. Patricks Crescent, which was nearly 60 years ago, that was £1 a week, mortgage payments.) We had a big garden. We had the half nearest the sea. My father was very keen and grew vegetables. And I was keen to be where my father was and I would go out with him and pull up the radishes and carrots and things.

Mother was a marvellous cook. She didn't bake bread but she made the most wonderful cheesecakes. They used to be in squares and came out like flaky pastry these cheese squares, and she was very, very good at apple puddings and she put the rind of a lemon in the crust. She put them on for a long while so they came out a lovely golden brown. She walked miles to get blackberries and sloes to bottle. All across the top of our dresser there used to be bottles of plums. She never wasted anything. She was a most generous person but she thought it quite wicked to waste any food or throw it away.

The Colonnade with the Coastguard Cottages on the higher ground behind, now the site of the De La Warr Pavilion. c.1930

When I was quite small I used to walk across from the coastguard cottages to the Marina shops. There was a little grocery shop called Millers & Bailey and I used to go across there to get brown eggs for my dinner you see. They were very nice to me there. I used to go to the Maypole for my mother before Sainsbury's was opened. I can remember going along the road saying, 'Best butter, 1/9d. a pound, best butter, 1/9d. a pound,' so that I didn't forget it! There was a big toy shop in Devonshire Road called the Devonshire Emporium. No-one seems to remember it but me. It was a big shop and it sold big toys like motor cars and tricycles and things that cost a lot of money. That was down the far end. Then of course there was the Home and Colonial next to the

Maypole. Then there was Wickens. Wickens was a lovely old shop. That was a grocer where I used to go sometimes, and in Sackville Road there was Durrants, that was an electrician and a plumbers. Then there was a library called Baxters. They also had toys, 1d., 3d., and 6d. toys in the window. Then there was a sweetshop where we used to buy Dreamland toffee at 1d. a bar (about 5 or 6 inches long). It used to last a long time, and aniseed balls, 20 for a 1d. and sherbet dabs and lemonade powder. I used to like the wool shops. The one I liked best was Harvey's in Western Road. Of course, later it was Harvey and Thorne but when I was a little girl it was Harvey's. Miss Harvey wasn't very big, about 4 ft.10 inches and I can remember going there (I was about 8) and I was quite short and she looked over the counter and asked me what I wanted, and I said I wanted some wool to make my father some socks. So she bought out some wool patterns and I asked her how much they were and she said 3d. an ounce. So I said to her, 'Are those the best wools?' And she said, 'Oh no, the best wools are 6d. an ounce.' So I asked how many ounces I would need and she said, '4 ounces.' So I said that as it was for my father's socks I would have the better one. In the event it didn't cost very much more because as it was better wool it

St. Barnabas Infants class. Phyllis Burl is standing beneath the window and has a bow in her hair. The building is now the Library.

went further. (I was taught to knit at St. Barnabas School when I was 8).

When I was five I went to St. Barnabas School. I actually had gone to school for one day before this. My mother had to go out and she hated keeping my sister off school so she wrote a little letter asking if my sister could take me to school with her for one day. They were quite agreeable. Of course my sister was a lot older and it wasn't like going to the infant school. It was very nice there at St. Barnabas and nice children too. There was Miss Watson who was qualified on the violin. After she gave up being a teacher she taught music. She lived in Linden Road. Then there was Miss Evans. She was very sweet. That was all there was in the infants and then when you were eight you went upstairs to the Girl's School. The boys went to St. Barnabas School in Reginald Road. I remember a lot about my junior school upstairs. We had plays. We were trying to get enough money to asphalt over the playground. You see if a child fell down and got a graze it got nasty pebbles in it. So we had concerts with a view to raising enough money. But we never got it and it was only when the Library took it over that it was asphalted.

My uncle in Croydon came to see me when I was 4 or 5, and he said had I got a big doll? I said yes, I had got a big doll. It was one my sister had made me. You used to buy a rag pattern and it was all printed on it and you used to sew all round . It was a big doll she had made me. I was very upset when I showed it to my uncle because he said, 'I don't think much of that, that's not a nice doll.' I said, 'It's a very nice doll.' But my uncle said, 'I'll send you a doll.' So when my father went to Croydon he bought back a very lovely doll. A beautiful doll with lovely eyes and lovely hair you could comb and lovely little teeth. My sister made some clothes for it for me. I kept it for years and years on a little oak chair. When I became a Sunday School teacher I realised that some of the children must have been fairly poor so I took the doll down to Chandler Road to some children who lived there and the little chair and the next Sunday I asked them if they liked the doll and they said, it was smashed to pieces. I never gave away any of my toys after that. I had a very pretty trug given to me by my uncle when I was about 5; I lost that.

Nearly all the girl's I knew at St. Barnabas went away when the war came. One of my friends lived at Cooden. Her father was the professional golfer at Cooden Beach Golf Club and I used to walk home with her sometimes. It was very desolate. We used to pick blackberries all the way along Cooden Drive.

I had 1d. a week pocket money. I didn't have to work for it. But when I was older my mother used to insist that my sister and me made Christmas presents. I made lots of presents, about 15 to 20 and used to get money to buy wool and things to make them I would go down to the Methodist Church on a Saturday and they had a Christmas Club and I used to take money down to this savings club from a lot of people and because I did this I'd get 3d. a week. I wasn't given the 3d. it was put on a card which I was given at Christmas time to buy the things I needed to make Christmas presents. I made gloves and hats and aprons and underclothes and bed-jackets and toys for the children (golliwogs and teddy-bears). And tapestry pictures.

When I was about 10, I suppose, the *Children's Encyclopedia* came out by Arthur Mee and it was really very, very good. It was fortnightly about 1/3d. My mother and father thought it would be a good thing for me to have and I learnt quite a lot from it. I was very keen on poetry and it had one section on poetry which I used to study and learn the poems. It had a section which told you how to make and do things and I made quite a lot from that. It taught you how to make potpourri and I used to go down to the park and collect the rose petals that had fallen down, and I used to make potpourri and it smelt lovely.

I can remember games I played when I first went to school. I remember my father bought me a sorbo ball. It cost 2/6d. which was a lot of money in those days but when you hit them on the ground they went up quite high. They were lovely balls. We used to play a game called Sevens' against the wall with the balls. Of course we used to play games in the school playground. But I didn't play many games because I had rheumatic fever which left me with a bad heart, so I wasn't allowed to play games. I can remember ever so well people saying you mustn't play games and you mustn't do this and you mustn't do that and at times I used to get quite wound up and I used to go away and run right along the seafront just out of frustration because I wasn't allowed to do anything.

We had a friend who lived quite near us who had two girls. One was a bit older than my sister and the other one was about 3 to 5 years older than I was. Their mother used to sometimes come along secretly with some frocks that she thought might be nice for me. My mother was very clever with her fingers and she used to make me frocks herself. Nightgowns and all that. I can remember one day I went to school and my mother said to me, 'I think that frock does look a bit shabby,' and when I came home at 12 o'clock she had gone out and bought some very pretty cotton material and made a frock and it was all ready for me to wear in the afternoon. She was very clever with the needle.

I went to Sunday School but they couldn't send me to Guides or anything because I couldn't join in any of the games. I went to Sunday School and after Sunday School we went into church and after church we went home. In the afternoon I went to Sunday School again and in the evening I went to church again.

I remember some Sunday School outings. We couldn't go very far in those days. We used to go to Pevensey and places like that. On one Sunday School outing I think, just before the war, we went to Goudhurst. Mr. Wimshurst, who had the chemist shop in Devonshire Road, who was mayor at one time, he was Sunday School Superintendent and he had a cousin who had a beautiful fruit farm at Goudhurst. But normally we didn't go far. Then of course we had the Christmas treats where people used to volunteer to help to get the teas ready for the children and then, according to how many times we had been to Sunday School, we would get prizes. I think the first time I hadn't been very much and I went to the Bran Tub. I think I got a book in the Bran Tub.

On Empire Day we had these streamers given to us which we used to have over our shoulders and a red, white and blue rosette pinned on us and we used to march round the playground then up to the corner of Marina and Sackville Road and there was a flagstaff there, and we used to salute the flag. That must have been going on for a long while. We

St. Barnabas pupils on Empire Day earlier this century, one of the girls is Milly Burl, the older sister of Phyllis. The girls are wearing their rosettes and carrying their decorated batons supplied by the school.

didn't have a holiday then I don't think. But we were a Church of England School you see, so on saints days the children used to go down to St.Andrews Church for a service and I think that was a half day. The children of non-conformist parents didn't go, they stayed at school and read their bibles.

I can remember the last day of the term at St. Barnabas School and we were having school assembly and we were singing the end of term hymn and I was feeling unwell and I can remember thinking, 'I mustn't be ill in the middle of this, I must last out the hymn.' But anyway I was and they took me out and my mother took me to Dr. Saville after a day or two and he sent me home immediately and I was in bed for about 3 months. I had rheumatic fever. My sister was very good to me. She bought me things I loved to eat but I couldn't eat hardly anything and the doctor said, 'She must eat or she won't live', and he said, 'Whatever she asks for, get it.' So my mother came up and asked what would I like to eat. I said that I would like an ice-cream. Of course they didn't sell them in the shops like they do now, so the only place she knew where you could get ice-cream was the St. George's cinema, because they used to have them in the interval. So she went along to the cinema and they said that they got them from the Cafe Royal in Devonshire Road. So my mother went to the Cafe Royal and said that she wanted an ice-cream for a sick child and so they let her have one. And I can remember it now. It was a block. It was pink and white and green and that was the first thing I had and that started me off eating again. When I was better I had to have tonics. It was quite an expense for my mother because it was a 6 oz. bottle and it only lasted four days and it cost 7/6d. And we had to pay for the doctor and the medicines. I left St. Barnabas when I was 12 to go to the Grammar School. I wasn't well when they had the Scholarship but my father and my mother paid for me to go. It wasn't all that expensive (£12 or £15 a year) but it was all the clothes and equipment that cost the money. Cookery and sewing you had to buy all the things yourself so it was the extras that cost the money.

I went on October 5th 1926 to the Grammar School. There were just 55 of us. Our lessons were Algebra, Geometry, Trigonometry, Arithmetic, History, English, Cookery, Needlework, Chemistry, Science, Latin,

First day at Bexhill County Secondary School for girls, subsequently the Grammar School and now the Sixth Form College. The headmistress was Miss Davis and her deputy Miss Poole on her left front row.

French and Scripture. The headmistress taught us Scripture and we had to learn quite large amounts of the Bible off by heart. She used to say that in later life it would come back to us and I think it does.

We were working toward Matriculation and the Cambridge Certificate but I was taken ill and had to go into St. Georges Hospital in London. When I came out I wasn't fit for a long while so I didn't take it that year. At that time there was a slump on and it was very difficult to get a job. When I was 16 I was offered a job so I took the job as I thought I might as well have a year's training instead of staying at school, although I loved school. So I didn't take my Matriculation. Another thing I was very sad about was that I was very fond of Art (that was another subject we were taught). We had a Miss Hoskins who had the Vita Studios in De La Warr Road on the corner of Fairmount Road. We used to take the Royal Society Examinations as we went up through the school and we got certificates. If you got a whole set of certificates through the school you could send them up to get a full certificate which if you wanted to go in for Art would be very useful. I saved all my certificates and then the last year it was Speech Day when we

Wimshurst the Chemist, now the site of Boots which took over this old established firm. c.1930

should have been taking our examination and I couldn't so they said I could take it at the beginning of the next term. Of course at that time I was at work and I wasn't allowed to take it then. They were much more strict in those days.

I worked at Collis the chemist. They were the people who worked at Wimshurst and when Mr. Wimshurst sold the shop to Boots it was thought that they would take the staff on but they didn't, they got rid of them. So they banded together and started Collis the chemist. It had only been going a year when I went there so I started as a trainee book-keeper. Of course there were a lot of private schools in the town and a lot of them came to Collis. I remember we had 900 accounts, so there was quite a lot to do. Some schools used to have not only the personal accounts of the children but they also had photography accounts as well. I worked from 9.00 a.m. till 1.15 p.m., 2.15 p.m. to 5.00 p.m., 5.30 p.m. to 7.00 p.m. on weekdays and 8.00 p.m. on Saturdays. We had Wednesday afternoon off, but not until after 2.00 p.m. All for 5 shillings a week as a trainee.

I was there for 10 years 'till the war. During the war the staff went down from 12 people to 3 and Mr. Collis wanted me to go away when the invasion scare started because he would have been on duty at the observer post. He wanted me to go away because he didn't want me to be on my own in the shop. So I went to my auntie in Wales and when I was there the shop was blown up and poor Mr. Collis was killed.

I was a Sunday School teacher and I went to church as well, so Sunday, was out for doing anything. In the week I suppose, well, I would come home and mother would read to us and I would knit and do embroidery and tapestry. And in the summer my friend and I went for walks, perhaps over the Downs at Eastbourne. Sometimes as far as Glynde. Occasionally we went to the De La Warr to see the operatic society perhaps a Gilbert & Sullivan opera.

We came up here to St. Patrick's Crescent when I was 19 and we've been here ever since.

My sister got married. She got married in 1933. My sister worked at Miller & Franklin's in St. Leonards Road. She was a secretary and she married the manager there, and I was the bridesmaid. It was my job to cut up the cake into pieces to post, but she said to me to cut up pieces for the workrooms at Miller & Franklin. I said, 'How many,' and she said, '100,' so you can see it was a big shop. It was on the corner where the Ministry is now. On the opposite corner and on the further corner. On one corner were hats and clothes and materials then the other side

Phyllis Burl was bridesmaid at her sister's wedding, the reception for which was held at the Metropole Hotel.

was china and glass and opposite side was furniture and furnishings and carpets and funerals, and they had a lot of houses up Wilton Road where the staff lived, lived in you see. It was the biggest concern in the town.

There have been many changes in Bexhill. Galley Hill was not built up when I was young. The West Parade wasn't built up. I can remember seeing wild flowers along there. And the other side, South Cliff, we used to play up there. There were what I thought were caves, but my friend says that there were dug out by Canadian soldiers in the 1914-18 war. I was very, very keen on wild flowers and I used to go up there and on the seafront hunting for wild flowers. There used to be yellow-horn poppies and lavender and all sorts of lovely things growing along the beach. I'm sure they don't grow there now.

The seafront was different to what it is now. It had little railings round and little borders of soil and it was thick with sea-pinks there, growing all the way around and going down to the sea. There were spindle trees and tamerisks and tree mallows and it was all very, very pretty. I think the paper used to sponsor competitions for making the best sandcastle. Mr. Fowler, a local man, used to have a Punch and Judy Show sometimes, but I don't think I went to it very often. I used to go along the front when the band was playing at night. The Colonnade was all lit-up, very pretty. The band-stand has gone now and a sort of semi-circle but when the band was playing and the deck-chairs were there it used to be roped off so you couldn't go across so you used to go at the back out on to this wooden deck to get to the other side. There was the Lawn which was near the Coastguard Station. That had an entertainment for children in the afternoon (a matinee) and an evening performance. There was also one called The Poppies in the Park and that had an afternoon entertainment and they used to have treasure hunts for children and then there was an evening performance for grown-ups. I went to one performance at the Lawn. I went with some family friends. They had a little girl who was a bit older than me and another little girl who was a bit younger, and the younger little girl was very attached to me and would always take my hand and a man on the stage asked for children to come up and sing you see. So the eldest girl went up and we were lifted up on to the stage, but the little girl wouldn't let go of my hand and I bashed my nose on the step and the next thing I knew I was sitting on a lady's lap. We sang:

> A,B,C,D,E,F and G,
> H,I,J,K,L,M,N,O,P,
> Q,R,S,T now it's nearly said,
> U,V,W,X,Y,Z.

We would be about 4 or 5 years old.

The Colonnade

The Pergola in Egerton Park.

I can remember very faintly the horse-drawn bathing machines. I can remember Mr. Buxton and Mr. Howes had bathing stations, and there were ropes to pull the caravan things down to the water's edge. I went into one of them one day. You undressed in them and then they were pulled down to the sea. Then you had your bathe then you got back in and you were pulled back up again. We used to go bathing, living so near the sea of course. We only had to run across the top of the Colonnade and down and we were at the sea edge, and we could see the sea from our windows. In fact when we had a storm my father used to have pebbles all over his garden the next day.

I think there were about 15 schools, private schools, in Bexhill. On Sunday after the church service the girl's schools, Ancaster House, Ancaster Gate, The Beehive and St. Bernards, the children all used to walk along the parade. It was quite a sight.

When I went to work my insurance card was with the Prudential and they paid for the medicine but you had to pay for the bottle (1d.) which you took back afterwards. They also paid for your dental care. I was very conscious of costing my parents a lot of money when I was ill because of the pills and that, which I had to have.

**Footnote:** *Phyllis Burl lived in only two houses in her entire life, the last for 64 years. Unfortunately she died in August 1997 and so never saw this book in print*

*The Grammar School was originally known as the Bexhill County Secondary School and is now the Sixth Form College. Entry from the state schools was by scholarship but fee-paying pupils were also accepted.*

# Joan Bush (née Warburton) born 1919

I was born in November 1919 over Warburton's shop in Town Hall Square, which was then 39, Station Road. The Fire Station was then at the bottom of Amherst Road, and my earliest recollection was the rocket which used to go off every time there was a fire. This always frightened me. The second recollection was the large fire which engulfed the furnishing store, Miller and Franklin's in St. Leonards Road. The General Post Office was also situated in Town Hall Square, at the lower end of Buckhurst Road.

When I was five I started school at Mountcroft which was in Parkhurst Road at the corner of Albany Road. The school was run by two lovely ladies, Mrs. Neighbour and Miss Hyde, and Mrs. Bryan Gipps used to come in each week to teach music and dancing.

In 1927 we moved to London Road and from my bedroom window I could watch the steam trains leaving the West Station for Sidley and Crowhurst. At the age of 10 I went to the Bexhill Girls County Secondary School in Turkey Road, and whilst waiting to catch the bus home we often picked wild roses and flowers in the hedgerow on waste ground before Southlands Road and the property around was built.

The shop of E. Warburton & Son above which Joan Bush, née Warburton, lived as a small child

In those days there were about 35 independent schools in the district so plenty to compete against. At the beginning and end of each term trunks used to be piled up from one end of Bexhill Central Station to the other. No wonder Bexhill Central Station needed such long platforms.

There were also four cinemas in the town. The Gaiety was at the bottom of London Road near the crossroads. St. George's in Town Hall Square, the Ritz in Buckhurst Road and the Playhouse in Western Road.

Whilst at school I remember the De La Warr Pavilion being opened, and the Metropole Hotel which stood beside it. This was bombed in the war and has now made room for a putting green.

Each year the 'Daily Mirror Eight' used to come and perform on the sea front, eight ladies doing their Health and Beauty exercises, also during August the C.S.S.M. (Children's Special Service Mission) used to meet on the beach every day by the Clock Tower.

Putting Green on the site now occupied by Clock Tower Court. c.1950

I also remember that during the summer months there was a steam train which left Birkenhead and called in at Bexhill Central Station in the late afternoon before it finished its journey in Margate.

At the beginning of the war in September 1939, I had just finished training at St. Christophers Nursery Training College in Tunbridge Wells. So I was sent to look after evacuees with the Brighton Nursery School which had evacuated with several London nurseries to Glyndebourne. We fortunately lived in the Opera House, with its lovely grounds for the children to play in.

Joan on the right with a colleague and three of the children

We slept in the Artists' dressing rooms, and as the toilets were underneath we had the job of potting the children upstairs and with buckets walked across the stage to the toilets below. You can guess how we young nurses enjoyed acting out this part.

After a time the school returned to Brighton and with two of the staff I was transferred to Bristol to an Anglo American home which housed about 80 evacuees from the East End of London. Another large manor house and grounds.

Here we were visited by Queen Mary and the Princess Royal as at that time they were at Badminton. A lot of scrubbing and polishing that day!

Syston Court, near Bristol. Visit by Queen Mary, the Princess Royal and the Duchess of Kent, 4th May, 1941. Joan is the sixth from the left.

During the Bath raids we had to find a lot of extra accommodation.

After two years I joined my old College at Tunbridge Wells, but by then the 'doodle-bugs' had started and we were forced to evacuate the children very hurriedly. We were sent to Llangollen, North Wales a haven of peace and quiet. For a time we lived on the outskirts and to get to town we used to take a horse drawn barge, but after a month we all moved into the centre of Llangollen, much to the nurses' approval!

At the end of the war some of us returned the children to their parents in London and we often wondered how they would settle down to city life after having a free run of the countryside.

Footnote: *Joan Bush now lives in Eastbourne. The firm is still operating in Town Hall Square, run by a fourth generation of the Warburton family.*

Warburton Stores at the bottom of Belle Hill were demolished in the 1960s when King Offa Way was built. (Photograph by courtesy of the Bexhill Observer).

# Norman Cook born 1915

I was born in Sidley in 1915 on August 9th. My mother was Gladys Wood, one of a family of eight and they lived in Gloucester. She came to Bexhill as a very young girl and started as a parlourmaid in the Beehive School at the bottom end of Dorset Road. My father was Harry Cook the son of George and Mary Cook. He had three brothers and four sisters. The family moved to Canada when my father was 17 leaving him to fend for himself. He lived for a while in digs in one of the old wooden houses in Belle Hill opposite the top of Amherst Road. After the family went to Canada he never saw them again.

Wooden buildings erected during the time of the Napoleonic wars and used by the King's German Legion, demolished in 1960s.

When my parents married my mother was 21 and my father was 22. My father was employed by F. Banks who were builders merchants in Holliers Hill, where he worked until he retired in 1954. Although he was officially employed by Banks, he only got paid when there was work to be done, then he got paid at the rate of 4d. an hour. Meals were determined by the amount of money he brought home at midday. One

Wednesday, which was the half-day for shops in Sidley, when he came home at dinner time (as it was then called) my mother asked him to pop down to Perrys, the grocer at the bottom of the road, to buy a tin of Fray Bentos for our meal and on the way down he got confused and came back with a bottle of Friars Balsam a poor substitute for our dinner!

Norman Cook 4 years 7 months in 1921.

I was born at 40 Preston Road at the top of Sidley Street and then we moved to 5, Sidley Street, a little house next to Lofts the butcher. I think I was about five when they moved from there to 26 Sidley Street and we lived there until the outbreak of War in 1939. I'm not sure when our house was built but it was probably at the turn of the century. There was a group of about forty houses which were terraced. The entrance through the front door which shared a small area with the next door house, led into a hall. Off the hall was what was known as the front room which seemed to be used only on Sundays and birthdays. The next room to this was the kitchen which was the main living room. In this room was a grate, coal-fired with an oven in which the meals were prepared. Beyond that was the scullery which had a sink for washing-up, and an old boiler which was brick-built with a white plaster coating, in which the laundry was washed each week, heated by a fire underneath. After being so boiled, the clothes were taken outside the house and put through a wooden roller mangle which stood in the back yard. There was also an outside lavatory, and a small garden which my mother tended and in which she loved to grow chrysanthemums and montbretia, as these were her favourite flowers. Inside the scullery was a small room called the larder, for provisions, next to which stood a small coal shed. We did not have a 'fridge or a telephone in those days. Upstairs there were three bedrooms, a small one at the back, which was mine and where I could see the sea from the window and the fireworks which were occasionally displayed in the Polegrove all this before houses were built and obscured the view. There was a middle room for guests and a front room for my parents.

The rent must have been quite nominal by today's standards as my father probably earned about £1 per week. In the early thirties he had the opportunity to buy the house for £150 but that was a fortune far beyond his reach. We had only gas lighting in every room with an incandescent mantle. This was very fragile when bought and was placed over the outlet for the gas, which when lighted would make the mantle glow. It was not until the late thirties that electricity came to our house. I gave it to my parents as a present. We also had a bath put into the back bedroom which also served as my bedroom. Baths were previously taken in an old tin bath in front of the fire. My mother cooked on a gas stove in the scullery. The house was heated from the grate in the living room which had a back boiler for hot water.

When I was about ten or eleven I remember doing a paper round for something like a shilling a week for Thomas, the newsagent in Sidley

A 'Tin-Lizzie' which travelled between Bexhill and Ninfield, via Sidley.

Street. That is the only job I remember having until I left school. I started off at the Infants' School run by the formidable figure of Mrs. Kimber and I can still see her, although I was only 3 when I went there, with her mortarboard, her gown and her stick and I can still, to this day, remember the nostalgic smell of chalk. I left there when I was about 5 years old and went to St. Mary Magdalen's School, near Bexhill Station. I think my parents thought that I would get a better education there, although in retrospect I don't think it made a great deal of difference. For although I enjoyed my school years the only things I truly learned were English, Geography, History and Arithmetic. Mathematics and languages were out of the question there as the curriculum did not include these subjects, but it gave me a good grounding in English. This school, although Roman Catholic, accepted non-Catholics. It was here also that I gained my love for sports. I can well remember the school lunches. As it was a two mile walk to school my mother used to pay sixpence per week which would buy me a bowl of tomato soup and some bread each day. On very rainy days I was allowed to go by bus from Sidley to Bexhill station. This cost a penny each way. Outside the Old Forge at Sidley (where Payless stood) was a stopping place for one of the old Carter and Lidstone buses which was called the 'Tin

Lizzie', and this used to take me to school. In those days before there were bells to signal for starting and stopping the bus, the method used was to bang on the side of the 'Tin Lizzie', once to start and twice to stop. I am sure we schoolboys prompted a lot of unofficial stops!

The games I remember at school were soccer, cricket and rounders. We also played marbles and conkers. I once had a '44er' which meant that my conker had defeated that many others. When the horse chestnuts (conkers) were in season a hole would be bored through the middle of one and suspended on a string. The conker had previously been hardened by soaking in soda water or baking in the oven. It was then dangled in front of one boy whilst the other boy would hit your conker with his, and play was alternate shots until one conker was broken. That was how the score mounted up. Other games I remember were floating matchsticks down the gutters in a sort of Oxford and Cambridge boat-race, and a very popular game called 'skatums'. To play this two of you would stand about six feet from a front door or a wall and flick cigarette cards from your two fingers towards the door to hit it, When it dropped to the floor then your opponent would skate his and if when falling it covered one or more of the cards on the ground, then he would claim those as his. Hence the name 'skatums'. In those days cars were few and far between so it was possible to play in the road, and most evenings the parents would sit on the walls by their houses and watch the children play games during the long summer months.

Hopscotch was played on the pavements where the squares would be marked out with chalk, and whilst hopping, the game was to kick a piece of slate from square to square. 'Grandmother's Footsteps' was another popular game. One child would stand on one side of the road with his back towards the other children, whose task was to creep across the road in an attempt to touch the 'Grandmother' who, by turning suddenly and without warning, would attempt to see any child moving. The penalty was to return to the start. Anyone making the full journey and touching without being seen would then become the 'Grandmother'.

Another game was between two teams on either side of the road who would select a saying like 'Lighting Sidley's Lamps'. One team would then come within a few feet of the other and give the initial letters, in this case 'L.S.L.', and mimic the action suggesting the answer. The other team would attempt to solve the puzzle and would shout out the answer, and if correct they would chase and try to catch any of the other team before they returned to base.

Our street lamps then were gas lamps and just before dusk a man would come round with a pole and switch the gas on and light the lamps. I cannot remember when the system was changed to electricity. I do remember, however, that Bexhill was known for the joke that for excitement they used to light their other lamp for Christmas.

Looking back I know that I had an extremely happy childhood, although one tends to remember the best parts and blot out the bad bits. Money was very short in those days and I well remember once when we had no money for food that I sold my pet rabbit to my friend, Willy Field, for one shilling and sixpence, and that enabled us to be fed for two whole days. As an only child there is always the danger of being spoiled, but what you cannot avoid is being given 100% attention. However this was counteracted by my parents pushing me first of all into the Cubs, then into the Scouts, on into the Cadet Force and eventually into the Army Territorial Service, so I always had lots of friends. In the scouting days I was very keen on morse and my mother particularly used to help me. We would get an old front door bell armature and when the hammer was removed, which gave the ring, it would emit a buzz instead, and by mounting these on separate boards connected by wires, my mother and I would transmit messages in morse between our bedrooms. Both my parents always found time to play with me.

As a Cub and Scout I went away to camp. Our Sidley Troop was run by a splendid man called Eric Eagling. He was a very gentle man from a very gentle family which lived in Laurel House near Catt's Forge which was opposite the Sussex Hotel. Mrs Eagling was a very charming old lady. She had three sons, I think, one of them being Skipper George, as I remember. He was also a Scoutmaster and a Priest too. He used to carve beautiful walking sticks. Also in our Troop were the Hobbs boys, Willie Field and Frank Deeprose (later killed at Dunkirk). I used to thoroughly enjoy the camps.

Norman Cook under canvas c. 1935.

Two sayings of my parents have guided me through my life. If things were not going right my mother would say 'Put it away for now and try again later and it will be all right in the end.' My father's homily was 'I think we will smile yet.' These sayings have stood me in good stead. My father served in the First World War as a Gunner in the Royal Artillery. He joined up originally with the old Volunteer Force in 1912, later to become the Territorial Army. He, with many other Sidley men, went off to War in 1914 and was invalided out in 1917. Up to the time that I was commissioned thirty years later, I wore the cap-badge he had worn throughout the 1914/18 War. The first conscious memory I have of my father was in 1917, when he was brought home wounded, to Netley hospital just outside Portsmouth, and being taken into the ward by my mother and finding myself being kissed by a strange man who wanted a shave. I was just two years old.

I always remember my parents being not only my parents but my friends too. My grandparents on my father's side lived in Canada and I do not remember any letters from them, but I do remember that in our sitting room in Sidley Street there were portraits of them on the wall. I do not think that there was any contact with them. My mother's father was still alive after the Second World War, having served in the First

World War as a very young soldier in France. He was a Sharpshooter as he was a crack shot and wore crossed rifles on his sleeve. He was in the wood-turning business making boats and such. My grandmother brought up eight children under very straightened circumstances and I would always go to the family in Gloucester for part of the school holidays. One of my mother's sisters, lived there too, my Auntie May, who later came to live in Sidley with my Uncle Frank. It was a long train journey to Gloucester on the old Great Western line. In my teens my friend, Harry Ponsford and I used to cycle to Gloucester for holidays. We used to average about 100 miles a day.

I was about 18 or 19 when I first began to help Harry Ponsford with the Wolf Cubs and later the Scouts. We had our headquarters in one of the warehouses over Warburtons in the Town Hall Square, over the archway that now leads to Sainsburys. We had to climb a rope ladder to get into the room. It was derelict when we took it over so we cleaned it up, broke up empty tea chests from the grocers and lined the walls, covering the joints with laths begged from builder's yards, and then painted the interior. Phyllis Bevan used to help me with the Cubs, later to have a distinguished war career herself, and has now returned to live in Bexhill. She has another distinction, she was my first girl friend!!

Our Wolf Cubs came from quite poor families on the whole, so to gain funds, Harry and I would buy old railway sleepers from the old West Station for one shilling and sixpence each. We would then saw them into convenient lengths and on one night a week the boys would chop the blocks into fire wood, take them around the houses at a shilling a bag, and in two years we had made enough money to equip the Pack and Troop with our own camping gear. I also used to beg offcuts of leather from the shoe repairers, and on another Cub night we would repair the boys shoes. I think that if the youth of today were engaged in such activities there would be less delinquents around the world. We used to go camping in a field at Ingram's Farm owned by a Mr. Christmas. This was near the old Sidley football field with its pond in the corner, then a big dip which we called the jungle, then our field was the one beyond that. I was the first to take Cubs to camp and at night we had prayers around the flag pole as the Union Jack was lowered. On one night at that point it began to pour with rain so we quickly got the boys off to bed and as I was walking round the tents picking up the odd sock etc., I heard one of the boys say to the others in the tent 'Akela forgot to say prayers tonight', and those boys knelt in their tent and said their prayers.

My interest in the Army began when I used to walk home from school, as an old wooden wheeled German gun from World War I stood on the Green near the New Inn at Sidley. I always felt a maddening excitement as I reached the Green and I can remember fighting my way from tree to tree to capture the gun single handed against a horde of Germans! I also remember a large tank on the seafront at the bottom of Richmond Road but I was never successful in capturing that! There was also an old sea mine there for a while but all of these disappeared as much-needed scrap iron during the war.

Sidley Green c.1926 where Norman Cook fought many a battle.

My life in Sidley as a boy was the very simple life as it was a very closely knit community. In towns one scarcely knew your neighbours but here in Sidley everyone was known by their first names. There was great friendship in those days. At Bexhill I recollect also the Kursaal, a wooden building stretching out to sea on wooden stanchions, and concerts and dances were held in it. During my dinner hour from school I would walk under the Kursaal and could always find pennies and halfpennies, and sometimes a silver sixpence, which had fallen through the wooden slats of the Pavilion floor.

In Sidley it is the tradesmen that I remember well. Teddy Mason was our milkman and he was always dressed impeccably in shiny leggings and boots, and in his pony and trap would be polished milk churns holding about 50 gallons of milk. When he banged on the doors we would come to him with our jugs and with long handled ladles he would measure out the required quantity of this creamy fluid into our utensils.

Bread was also brought to the door. The two bakers I remember were Hoads and Pankhurst. They both had flour mills, one in Camperdown and one near the Downs. The fresh baked bread at about twopence a loaf was carried in baskets covered with a cloth. Both mills are now sadly gone, hidden under building sites. The Pipeclay man was a regular Saturday visitor. Pipeclay was a fairly soft white chalk, clay like stuff, which the mothers would wet and then whiten their doorsteps. It was, of course, the same material from which clay pipes were made. These cakes of clay were one penny each.

Also on Saturday mornings the children would wait eagerly for the Banjo Man. Dressed in a straw hat and a coloured blazer, he always stood by the lamp post outside our house and play and sing popular songs. My mother would take me to the cinema, St. Georges, in the Town Hall Square one afternoon a week. Often they would show in later years the opening of the cinema and we could see my mother carrying me as a small curly headed boy, across the street. Great excitement that! We were in there once when a notice on the screen asked my mother to go to the box office, where we learned that my father had broken his leg at football.

My father was a very natural games-player, both football and cricket. At football he had a trial with the Sussex Colts. He played for Sidley F.C. along with 'Rooster' Ransome, Alan Featherstone, the Green brothers, Ginger Walters the goalkeeper, and many others. He played cricket for both Sidley and Bexhill, whereas I played for the Athletic and Parkhurst Clubs. Sometimes our teams met each other, but he was always the much better player. He excelled in both batting and bowling. He bowled left-handed and batted right-handed, whereas I played the opposite way to him. It was through him I gained my interest in sport. As a very young boy my mother would take me to watch him play at Glovers Lane or Haddocks Hill (the old Carey's ground) and the Polegrove. The Polegrove used to be the old rubbish tip but was levelled off and the playing fields made 80 years ago. My mother was one of several ladies who opened up the tea hut at Glovers Lane and helped with the scoreboard. Everyone used to get involved in local activities like that.

That brings me to the pageants we were involved in during the Thirties. Every year a procession of floats would parade around the town. They were drawn by horses in polished harness and glittering brasses which jingled as they moved and the villagers would ride on the floats dressed in various costumes. My mother built up a reputation as depicting Britannia. Her costume was made of white muslin, her shield was made from a wooden hoop belonging to Ivy Furner and covered with a Union Jack. The helmet was made from a fireman's helmet belonging to the local Fire Chief, Mr. Bodle, which was painted with gold paint and a plume attached. We always made our own costumes from bits and pieces. I was usually a page boy with long hose, a doublet and a large hat with a feather on it. In 1932 we had the Battle Abbey Pageant. Gwen Lally was a lady, well known nationally, who ran pageants around the country. She gave each village around Battle a part of the 1066 history to arrange, and the villages, including Sidley, set to to make costumes and fittings for their part of the Pageant which was called '1066 AND ALL THAT'.

For the pagent Sidley was to produce the funeral of Sir Anthony Browne, once the owner of Battle Abbey. My father carried a forty foot banner depicting his Arms, my mother was a village wench and I was

Gladys Cook, mother of Norman, dressed as Britannia c.1920

the Abbot of Jumiere. The play was enacted for two weeks and began with the pastoral scene of Battle with sheep and foxhounds parading, and then moved to the battle between the Normans and Saxons. The Normans appeared, some on horseback and advanced on the Saxons in their prepared positions on top of the hill of Senlac. Twice on Wednesdays and Saturdays and once every other day, the battle was fought out between some 200 men. According to history, the Normans could not displace the Saxons and so pretended to withdraw from the field bringing the Saxons out to give them chase. Then the Normans turned and drove the Saxons to defeat. The battle took 45 minutes and after the first week local inter-fighting started to take place and history was in danger of being re-written by the Saxons defeating the Normans! Gwen Lally was shouting through her megaphone for the Saxons to withdraw, but they would not. Dressing stations had to be set up behind the hessian screens for the actual wounded to be treated. There was great rivalry between the villages, but I cannot remember a lot of actual violence. I do recall a man called Putnam leaving the Pelham Hotel drunk and arguing with his son who was trying to get him home. The father was pushed over by the son and he struck his head on the ground and died. The son was on a murder charge and my mother raised a sum of money from the village to pay for young Putnam's defence, but he was found guilty of manslaughter and went to Lewes jail for a number of years.

The first policeman I remember was a Mr. Butler Brown and later a Mr. Perry. I used to push his baby out in a pram for sixpence. That was very useful and with my pocket money I bought my first football, and going up to the top of Sidley Street to kick the ball around a waste piece of land, I kicked it over the hedge onto Mr. Ransome's allotment. He was a formidable man with a long brown beard and when I asked if I could have my ball back he answered 'Yes,' but before he threw it back he stuck his knife into it. My father went to tell the policeman but nothing came of it.

I remember Mr. Buxton from The Sussex very well, first of all he owned the pub (now the Sussex Hotel). He was a tall thin man and was also the chairman of Sidley Football Club for which my father played for many years, and I still have several medals he won for various Cup Competitions. There was a snooker table at the Hotel and my father taught me to play. I remember going there one day to play with him and we heard Mr. Buxton ('Buckie' as he was known) using every swear word in the English language because he was trying to clean the snooker balls in a bucket containing boiling water and ordinary soda, and all the colour came out of the balls and we were left with 22 white balls, so there was no snooker that day!

We went on rambles too. At the top of our road was Sidley Wood made up mainly of sweet chestnut trees with an enormous holly tree in the middle, which nearly every girl in Sidley had her name carved in the trunk or branches over the years as it was an easy tree to climb with low hanging branches. In the young chestnut tree groves we had rival gangs who would clear away the undergrowth and bend over the young saplings and fix them with wire to make a camp in which we could hide from rival gangs. Fred Woodley was my opposite gang leader and we would pretend to have fights with bows and arrows but no one ever got hurt.

Many years later after I was married and had a four year old daughter, we had gone up to the woods to play just before Christmas. She was the beautiful young princess imprisoned in the castle and I was the knight who would rescue her. She ran off to hide and I had a long walking stick which I put between my legs and pretended to be galloping to find her and rescue her from the wicked knight and his dragon. One day, with no daughter in sight, I was galloping happily along the path and came round the corner to see two elderly ladies coming towards me. They were amazed to see this six foot man in his thirties galloping along on a stick! As I passed them I said, 'Happy Christmas' and disappeared as quickly as I could. On the next Sunday I was walking along Bexhill front with my wife and daughter and who should be coming towards me but the same two ladies. I could imagine them saying to each other, 'That's him'. I gave them a beaming smile as we passed!

I can remember going carol singing as a boy with my father and one or two others, when my father would play the carols on his mouth organ (which I still have) whilst we sang, and we would collect a few shillings by doing that. Carol singing always reminds me of the Salter family. They lived a few doors down from us and Lesley, known as 'Nibs', and his brother Reg and his father who had good voices would tour the area and sing most beautifully. They were well known by the musical concerts they gave and the plays such as 'Dogs of Devon' etc.

I do not recall ever having a Christmas tree but it must have been near a Christmas when I was ill with measles, and I can well remember the delight in waking from a sleep, lying on the sofa in the living room, when my eyes focussed on a colourful Christmas stocking hanging on the wall with some sticky sweets and little tin scales, and it truly was a marvellous sight. Children only got presents at Christmas and birthdays and it usually turned out to be much needed clothes, but I am sure there were other things with which to play. In those days new clothes were a luxury, and my mother used her sewing machine and knitting needles to make most of our clothes. She was always very busy. She did not work outside the home until many years later when she worked in the Tennis office in Egerton Park, and not until I was well grown up.

I went to school until I was fourteen and I started work at Wickens in Devonshire Road, first as an errand boy on a carrier bicycle with an enormous basket both front and back, and later as an assistant in the shop. It was good training in learning about human nature. My cousin, Tom Cook, also worked there. He was actually my father's second cousin (my grandfather's brother's child) and was a lot older than I. He had been in the Occupational Army of the Rhine after the First World War.

We were in the shop one Saturday evening when I saw a woman take a small hock of bacon from a stand, pop it in her basket and walk out without paying. I told my cousin about this and we set a trap for her on the following Saturday. We had a metal three-tiered stand with a plate on each level in which we put the small hocks at sixpence each and tied a long piece of string to the one remaining hock when she came in. From either end of the counter we watched her pick up the hock and put it in her basket and begin to walk away. When she was about three yards away, she dragged the whole stand off the counter on to the floor. We never saw her again.

When I first began work at Wickens I was sent round to the big hotels around Knole Road to take orders, and Mr. Wickens would give me one shilling a week if I used my own bicycle. This was quite a bit as I was earning only 7/6d. per week anyway. During winter months when business was not so good he dropped that to 6d a week for my bike. On my first week there he told me to sweep out his office and I found a half-crown under his chair. I took it to him and said, ' I have found this under your chair', and he replied, 'Yes, I know, I put it there'. So I passed my first test. I was there until the outbreak of war in 1939.

In 1935 I joined the Territorial Army. I always wanted to join the Army but thought that the fact I wore glasses would prohibit me from so doing. However, one day, watching the Armistice Day Parade in Bexhill and seeing the local Royal Artillery contingent on parade with their polished field-guns towed by horses, and their uniforms with jingling spurs, I was hooked and went to the Drill Hall on the Downs to enlist. I joined as an ordinary Gunner attached to the Signal section. I later rose through the ranks to Sergeant and was later commissioned, and, after the War returned to raise and command the first post-war Territorial Battery in the same Drill Hall where I had enlisted in 1935. Our Battery went to France with the British Expeditionary Force early in the War, and after Dunkirk I was commissioned and went to Burma for four and a half years.

Norman Cook T.A. Camp c.1937. 231 Battery R.A. 58 Field Brigade.

I was always able to talk to my parents about problems and I always got good advice from them. My mother was the disciplinarian in the family and I think this is the same in most families as the mother has to cope with the children all day, whilst the father comes home after work and plays with them, and punishment cannot be administered too long after the event. Hence the mother bore the brunt of it. Both were very firm with me when necessary but I was never beaten. The worst thing she did was to smack my legs, never my head. Just up the road from where we lived was a little corner shop run by a Miss Knowles. It was a very old-fashioned shop even for those days. It sold sweets and groceries, and corn and the like, and a little bell tinkled at the top of the door when it was pushed open. I can actually smell that little shop as I write these words; it was a smell of spices and biscuits and fresh bread. I can remember my mother coming home one day to find me eating some biscuits and when she asked me what I was eating and I told her, she asked me where I got the money to buy the biscuits from Miss Knowles. I said, 'Off the mantelpiece'. She said that the money was not mine to take and that I had stolen it, and I was to take the biscuits back to get the twopence refunded, which I did as Miss Knowles was a very understanding little lady.

On another occasion I had been playing ball in the street when I accidentally kicked my ball through the front floor window of Mrs. Boniface's house, so I dashed indoors and sat down. Whenever I did that my mother would say, 'Well what have you done now?' and when I told her she said that I must go and tell her and say that my father would repair the window when he got home. I can vividly remember going up to the front door of the house and saying, 'Please Mrs. Boniface, I broke your window'. 'I know', she said, 'I saw you do it!'. These are two instances where my parents taught me responsibility and discipline.

My father used to smoke a great deal and my mother just loved chocolate, but when my father had a chest complaint he gave up smoking overnight and my mother took to smoking and gave up sweets, which my father then took a liking to. We were fortunate not to have tragedies in our family other than grandparents dying of old age.

I don't think we ever went away on holiday as a family but we went for lots of picnics when the weather was fine. There was an area called 'the Mount' and 'the Dell' over the fields from Glover's Farm, and it was close enough to home for my father to go back to make a pot of tea and bring it to the picnic site. We also spent a lot of time on the beach. I was never a good swimmer as I much preferred the countryside to the sea.

When Harry Ponsford and I were Scouting, our holidays were spent on cycling tours when we would go via the coast for Harry's benefit and back via the country for me. Our tent was carried on his handlebars and the mackintoshes on mine, and we both had pannier bags on the back of the cycles for our food and clothing. We would cycle most of the morning, stop to have our dinner and sight-seeing, then cycle on until late afternoon, camping down before dusk. We would average 100 miles a day doing this. Once when we cycled to Gloucester my aunt and uncle came out some 10 miles to meet us at a hill called Birdlip, a very steep and winding hill at the top of which they gave us some local cider which was nicknamed 'Stunnan'. After a couple of glasses of that we knew why it had such a name as it turned the spindle of my bicycle into a corkscrew and I do not remember riding the last ten miles.

Sunday was always a different day at home as although we did not go to Church, my father was home for the day. I did, however, go to the Baptist Chapel in Sidley Street called Haddon Hall. I went there because it was handy for home and I liked the happy hymns to which one clapped hands. You had a card called a Star Card and it received a star every time you went, and you were given presents at the end of the year relating to the number of stars you had collected. I was given the first Bible I had ever had, with little cut-out parts to find chapters more easily. Mr. Hoad was our teacher and minister. Haddon Hall had an old corrugated tin roof and was about 25 yards from my back garden, and my mother would go there to play whist in the afternoons. I was quite a young boy when I used to pick up clods of earth and throw them to make a noise on the tin roof. One day, when my throwing was less than accurate, I threw a clod through the glass window and my mother said to herself, 'Norman!'. No supper for me that night.

One of the sights to fascinate me was to watch the horses being shod at the forge where the buses used to stop, and where Payless now stands. There we children would watch the bellows making the fire roar, watch the iron shoe turn from grey to red and then white heat, and then the moment supreme when the shoe was put on the horse's hoof and it would give out that delightfully pungent aromatic smoke. We would visibly wince when the nails were hammered home, not knowing that the horse could not feel a thing. I can also remember the thatchers at work as at that time a lot of houses still had thatched roofs.

High Street, Sidley c.1912. A triangle of trees divided All Saints Lane from Ninfield Road.

A sight seldom seen today but commonplace then, was the stooks of corn in the fields placed in sheaves to dry. It was a splendid picnic spot. I seem to recall long hot summers from my youth but I can also remember having my nose against the windows whilst the rain teemed down, but on the whole I feel the seasons were much more separate in those days. One project I remember doing was to make a map of Crowhurst Marshes. This was an area where the old Viaduct used to stand, taking the trains from Bexhill to Crowhurst. It had many dykes crisscrossing it but with a 100 foot length of rope I mapped it out, marking in the crossing places as the streams were too wide to jump without the danger of wet feet. These streams would freeze in the winter and when several of us were over there one year, Jimmy Batkin, who was one of our Scouts, fell through the ice and was totally immersed. We put an old gate across the river and got him out, and as his clothes began to freeze on him we ran him all way the home, but he still became ill with pneumonia and landed up in hospital. I do not think I ever felt really cold as I have always had a good deal of blubber to keep me warm.

Sidley Station only operated for sixty years. The site is now a service station. Trains ran from Bexhill West Station via Sidley to London.

Local shops were always a treasure trove for small boys, just looking in the windows and seeing all the luscious sweets and toys. Sometimes when I was with my Uncle Frank he would ask me what I liked in the window and then he would buy it for me, but that did not happen very often. Slade's sweet shop was a favourite haunt of mine, just around the corner from Perry the grocer. Mr. Slade was a fusty dusty old man; his shop was fusty and dusty too, because I can remember my father taking me in to buy a quarter of a pound box of chocolates for my mother's birthday. The one we wanted was in the window with the lid off. Mr. Slade got it out, blew the dust off the sweets, put the lid on it and wanted to sell it to us. He taught me how to play chess. We would sit behind his counter when I was about eight or nine amongst the array of gob stoppers and lollipops and bulls eyes, but he never gave me any.

I used to get sixpence a week pocket money, about 2½ new pence today. I well remember a lesson my mother taught me when I was about 11. I had asked for my pocket money early because there was a fair in the village. When I got home my mother asked where my sixpence was and when I told her I had spent it at the fair on the machines and she asked me what I got for it. I opened my hand and showed her a few sticky sweets which the crane had picked up for me instead of the watch I was after. Then she said, 'Which would you rather have, those sticky sweets or your sixpence?' I hopefully replied that I would rather have the sixpence and she said, 'Well, bear that in mind the next time you go to the fair'. Another lesson learnt.

Then there was Bristows the cycle repair shop where there was always the smell of rubber solution. Mr. Bowditch also had a sweet shop on the corner of Sidley Street. There was Dobsons too, the draper and grocer. Here again I was taught a very good lesson. Wilfred Dobson was a friend of mine and we had a habit of hanging on the back of lorries passing through the village. Wilfred was doing just this one day when he slipped and his leg went under a wheel, stripping the flesh off from thigh to ankle, and my mother took me to see him lying in the road and saying, 'That is what happens by hanging on to lorries'. That incident occurred at the top of what is now Buxton Drive but at that time there were just two large green gates there, with fields beyond where you were able to get to London Road, which at that time ceased in the vicinity of Cambridge Road. The Post Office was in Perry's shop and there was Arscott the Baker almost opposite the bottom of Sidley Street. The fish and chip shop was owned by George Hall, and was placed between Arscotts and the Sussex Hotel, where we used to buy two pennyworth of crackling. These were the bits and pieces left over when the fish was cooked. It was cheaper than buying the fish although we sometimes had a fourpenn'oth of fish and a pennyworth of chips. These were served in newspaper and when salt and vinegar were added the aroma was out of this world. Its the only way to eat fish and chips. Edie Ransome had a corn shop in Sidley Street selling not only corn but pickles in enormous jars, and you took your own jam jars to get two pennyworth of piccalilli or red cabbage. Our diet was enhanced by a lot of fresh vegetables grown by my father in his allotment, firstly in Ringwood Road and then at the bottom of Preston Road by the woods.

A Saturday morning treat was the arrival of the rag and bone men with their carts to collect clothes and jars and newspapers, for which they would give us either balloons or a home-made windmill on a stick, apart from a few pence for my mother.

So this narrative sums up what has always been to me a very happy childhood, where I enjoyed having loving parents and good friends. Sadly, many of the boys I grew up with lost their lives in the War, and when visiting All Saints Church in Sidley after the War I was saddened by the names I read on the Memorial hanging in the Church, and I penned these words:

## Men of Sidley

*Men who were boys when I was a boy, hid now in Death's dark cloak*
*Remembered still in a Sidley Church, carved names in mellowed oak.*
*Games which we as children played were childish games of war*
*Wooden guns and wooden spears were all the arms we bore.*

*Langmore, Rogers, Ridgeway, Tidd, remember those who died.*
*Izzard, Errey, Fuller, Beal, remember them with pride.*

*Boys who were men before their time, their manhood forged in fire*
*Gave their lives that we might live, to this do men aspire.*
*Some ventured forth to foreign lands, across a hostile sea*
*And came back not to those who loved, but became a memory.*

*Nervard, Oaten, Barnes and Grant, do not these men forget.*
*Williams, Verrall, Scotcher, Croft, their names re-echo yet.*

*With clear bright eyes and measured tread they left their native land*
*To die in jungle, desert, swamp, or Dunkirk's bloody sand.*
*Their heads held high and hearts aglow, they faced the cannon's roar*
*As Nelson, Drake and Marlborough did, in far off days of yore.*

*Birnie, Baker, Christmas, Bush, their graves are scattered wide.*
*Duncan, Deeprose, Haddow, Hodge, full high their glories ride.*
*Stoner, Vidler, Ellis, King, proudly their praises pen.*
*For Sidley is as Sidley was because of Sidley men.*


**Footnote:** *On his return from war service Norman Cook raised the first post-war Territorial Battery in Bexhill. He retired to the town in 1978 where he is still active as Welfare Officer to pensioners of the International Distillers and Vintners Company.*

# Peter Evenden born 1920

My name is Peter Henry Evenden and I live at 1, Gatelands Drive Bexhill. I was born on the 18 December 1920 at 60 Sackville Road.

My father was a draper and occupied the ground floor with a drapers shop and we, naturally, lived in the two upper floors above the shop.

I was the first born, my sister Sheila was born 4 years later and she still lives in Bexhill.

My father Henry Percival was born in Penshurst in Kent, the family were Kentish people, and moved to Sussex after he was born. He was born in 1888.

He came to Bexhill in 1912 and married my mother shortly after, some time between 1912 and 1915. Before the 1914-18 War, he was about 25. My mother came from Eastbourne and they met at Evendens.

His father set up the shop. He had the village shop in Herstmonceux for many years, then retired to Springfield Road, Bexhill, aged forty. He opened the shop in Sackville Road in 1912 together with my father. My father was apprenticed to Miller and Franklin, then one of the larger drapery people and my mother was apprenticed to Evenden's, a department store in Cornford Road, Eastbourne, not a close relation.

A draper is a man who sells ladies clothes often called 'a draper and milliner,' they sold hats as well. They used to sell all ladies clothing and underclothes, uniforms for living-in maids, corsets and even equestrian knickers, with stout elastic just above the knee.

The shop was on the right, near the sea. It is now a fish and chip shop. My father ran the shop till he was 85 when was brought to his knees by VAT; he couldn't cope with this in the early 70s. He was nearly floored by decimal currency but went on pricing in £sd, in sheer cussedness.

At first my grandfather lived above the shop then he moved into one of the new houses in Woodville Road and my father and mother moved in.

The first floor had 4 rooms, second floor 3 rooms, bathroom and wc. I had my own bedroom. We had one sitting room and a very big

Peter Evenden's father outside his shop in Sackville Road.

kitchen which worked as kitchen/dining room. Two of the top rooms were stock rooms.

We didn't have servants. I had a kind of part-time nanny for a bit and ladies came in to do some cleaning. My mother did most and from about 1930 she sometimes helped in the shop. She liked to do that.

I was in and out of the shop as a child and played in the street, it was safer in those days. Sackville Road property was largely built as shops. Western Road was built as residential and became shops.

I saw quite a lot of my grandfather and he gave me 3d. to trim his lawn which he had mowed. My grandfather grew beautiful lettuces and my grandmother baked her own bread.

My father rented the rooms from my grandfather who served in the shop till about 1920. I have a memory that in my teens we paid a rent of about £90 pa. That would be about 1930.

Bexhill Swimming Baths in Egerton Park before the alterations which took place in the 1950s.

Swimming was a big thing in our life when I was 8, 9 or 10. I can't remember when I learnt to swim but it was a family tradition that we went to the sea or the swimming baths every morning from the date of my father's birthday on 28 May. If the tide was up we went to the sea, if too low to the baths. The whole family, before school. It was standing drill. We had to have the first swim on the 28th May and I've always loved swimming. My mother wore a costume with legs down to just above the knee and short sleeves, black usually or black with red stripes. A mob cap, a rubber one. My sister wore a costume, and the men wore longer legged costumes, not trunks. We often went as a party with friends. The Wallaces, Tom Wallace, a fairly well known builder in the town and his family.

My recollection is that my parents took no newspaper other than the *Daily Express* and no magazines except the *Draper's Record*.

We didn't take holidays at all. The shop was the dominant thing. The shop was open till 6.30 or 7 and 9 o'clock on Saturdays. Wednesday was firm early closing. From the time he came back from World War I until the day he died the only time my father didn't sleep in his own bed was on my wedding night in Northampton in 1942. He would have worried about the shop. My mother went to Tunbridge Wells sometimes for a few days with her sister He lived only for the shop till he was 85 when the shop was a dead loss. It was his life. When he left, he lived another 10 years, but he got deaf, also could not see very well and died within himself. It was his life. I don't know what the pull was but I think it started because he was on a treadmill and he had to survive, he got into the habit, then he didn't know any alternative.

Father didn't have any hobbies. He went out to buy a wireless in the 20s and came back with a motor car. A Wolseley, 2 seater with a dicky. He kept it for 4/5 years and then bought a wireless set and got rid of the motor car.

At about 5 I went to "Mountcroft", an independent school in Parkhurst Road run by Mrs. Neighbour and her assistant Miss Hyde, a mixed school. We started off by learning to do pot hooks, I didn't understand why we had to do them, they were J's forwards and backwards. I learned to write copper plate and to write a copy book and sepia drawing and all kinds of interesting things and along the line to read and write and my tables. I had a desk (a longish desk for 4/5) with ink wells and sat on a fixed bench. An ink monitor collected up the wells

wells and sat on a fixed bench. An ink monitor collected up the wells and cleaned them. We came home to lunch. Lunch was a family meal the main meal of the day. My father shut the shop for an hour.

We used to walk there and when I came home I walked down Parkhurst Road and then down Sackville Road till I got opposite the shop and then I would stop and shout and Dad would come out of the shop so I could cross the road. I doubt if you could get away with that in Sackville Road today.

We ate as a family except for tea which I had when I got back from school. Quite often our evening meal was late. Sometimes we had supper before we closed the shop.

My father did his books in the flat and used to like to go down to do his ordering and cashing up. He had a mahogany cash desk, three sided, with an arched hole where you could pay a cashier but that was replaced by modern tills where you wrote on bits of paper. Greens, the other larger draper down the bottom end Sackville Road had the cash on the overhead wires which held the money and spun along the lines, as did other big shops. I always wished my father had the same, like Miller and Franklin and Bobby's and Beals in Eastbourne.

The shop of George Green at Nos. 24, 26 and 28, Sackville Road, friendly rivals of H. P. Evenden

was no ill will. My sister was friends with their children. If Greens had been shut for a day my dad would have been pleased, that's all.

Not all my friends went to the same school.

I took the entrance examination just before I was 10 to get into the new grammar school, which I duly did, in 1930. It wasn't a very difficult exam. Not many children didn't pass. I had to write about a horse and I told my parents I'd written that a horse is an animal with a leg at each corner, having 4 in number, and they weren't very impressed but I passed just the same. I don't think you had to be very clever, the school just wanted pupils.

I was very happy there. It was great . It was new. Proper school masters and boys. I liked it a lot. Especially sport and football. I don't think there was any social stigma between the grammar and independent schools, we played Rowbrough and others at cricket, not within the community that I was conscious of, not within the social level I was living. In the middle class level it wasn't there. The grammar school was more rigid, there was more discipline and each master had his own method of torturing one if one did something wrong. Then there was the cane as the ultimate deterrent. We didn't live in fear.

We had to wear uniform, that was very strictly applied. We had to wear a cap or boater. Speech day was special and we had to wear stiff collars. Grey flannels and grey shirts and grey jacket with red tie and red cap, mackintosh. Slacks in the summer and red blazer. Boaters doubled as a frisby. The boys didn't have a gym till '38 or '39 but we did plenty of PT, team games and athletics. The girls had a gym.

If there was a really nice day in the summer they would spring a swimming parade and that was quite an event. The whole school stopped, lined up and marched down to the beach to swim without exception and thoroughly enjoyed it. Not the girls, they were totally separate. A hedge divided the playing grounds; boys were not allowed within a metre of the hedge. Miss Davis was the headmistress and there are lots of stories about her. One was when Carey's sent up a mower to mow pulled by a horse and after it had walked up and down a few times Miss Davis went mad and they were told to replace it with a mare

times Miss Davis went mad and they were told to replace it with a mare at once. We didn't find the girls attractive. I wasn't interested in them. They were sombrely dressed with black gymslips and black knickers and stockings and white blouses, black velour hats. They weren't interesting, they didn't play football.

I didn't have a weekend job as such, maybe I've been workshy all my life. I got 1/- pocket money. I did some deliveries for my father, Saturdays, on my bike, but not a lot.

Sunday was choir. Two services, matins and evensong, and then I became a server. Originally at St Andrews, in Wickham Avenue and then the congregation went and built St Augustines, in Cooden Drive, so I moved when our choir-master moved. We didn't go to church as a family. I got into the choir on the behest of my grandfather who was a sidesman. My sister decided to join the Methodist's Sunday School.

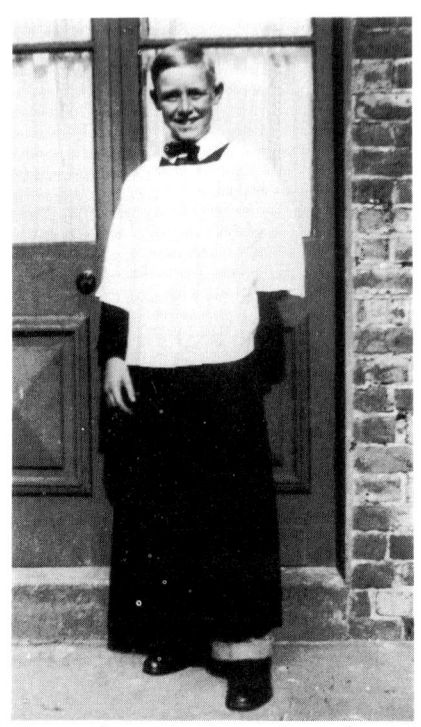

Peter Evenden in 1933. He was first a choirboy at St. Andrew's and then transferred to St. Augustine's in Cooden Drive.

St. Andrew's Church in the snow in 1920. Note the tram wires.

My father was tall with aquiline features, clean shaven. My grandfather had an Imperial beard. My father wore a suit and tie with a highish collar.

I didn't consider my parents strict. There was no talk of that in those days. There was nothing to stay out for. I had a canoe I had saved up to buy which cost 25/-. It took a lot of collecting, and I spent all summer evenings with that on the beach, there till it got dark.

You could say what you thought at table, our conversation was free. He wasn't a Victorian father in any way. I think his attitude to the world was guided by Lord Beaverbrook as much as anything else. My mother helped in the shop but didn't miss not having a career. As a woman of her time she accepted you worked for your family after marriage. Her sister who remained a spinster became a company secretary for Caffyn's. My mother never envied that career structure. She didn't get involved in voluntary work. She was quite happy as long as she had 25 cigarettes a day and she wasn't very interested in clothes. You don't know everything about your parents, you only know what they chose to show you, but they seemed a happy pair. I think I talked to her more, I was meant to be like her side of the family.

Besides my grandfather my godfather was an influence. Herbert or Bert Heather, manager of Hall and Co. in Bexhill. He was a great sportsman and joined us for our family swim sometimes. I admired him. He was a founder member of Rotary so I'm second generation in a way. I was expected to join his firm so left school after taking school certificate but was turned down on medical grounds with eczema. So I had to look for another job - so long as it wasn't drapers, I didn't want to go into my father's shop.

They considered eczema not suitable for a builder's merchant so I had no job and thats how I came to go into estate agency. In 1938 I joined Lionel Heather. There were five lads and we all soon joined one of the forces. I went to the TA, the old 58 Field Regiment, and by 1st September 1939 he was left on his own. So I only had a year there.

When I started at Lionel Heather I got 2/6 a week, then by Sept '39 it was 5/-, about 5 packets of cigarettes I didn't give my parents anything. They felt I was still learning. I started a correspondence course in surveying. Then I went into the army where they paid me 2/- a day - 14/- a week; I reckoned I was made.

My sister was still at school at the girls grammar school which was evacuated to Letchworth. Then she became a land girl and then joined the WRNS. My sister has never married. I met my wife as a military policeman in Reading when she was in the Womens Auxillary Air Force. We married in Northampton in early '42, the kiss of death as then she was moved to Herefordshire. We couldn't set up home at once but happily it all survived.

The population of Bexhill had largely removed on account of the danger and the sea front was blocked off with barbed wire.The old Metropole was occupied by the RAF who burnt the top two floors off it. The Luftwaffe training school was at Rouen and it was said that part of their passing out test was to go over to Hastings or Bexhill and drop a bomb and fly back, and it seemed to happen. One's parents lived in continual danger. It must have been miserable. Town very quiet apart from the advent of Spike Milligan, who was stationed in the town, and his band; this was the biggest event of the our war. Rotary members George Woodvine, Stanley Courtney and Tom Gardener (later founder of the Association of Bexhill Citizens), organised dances at the Pavilion. My father got involved as an ARP warden and went fire watching and read meters to increase his income.

After the war I came back and re-joined Lionel Heather. I was a Captain in the army and had made my professional mark as a soldier but I had no qualifications. Lionel had been working for war damage and examining war damaged properties. and took me back. So I learned about dealing with such buildings and pursued my professional exams by correspondence. We lived in a flat over Barclay's Bank, which Lionel had taken; the rent was part of my salary. We had three rooms and one daughter was born in 1944. I was paid £5 per week which was a bit of a comedown.

Bexhill Athletic Club Band playing at St. Peter's Hall, date unknown.

Bexhill differs from before the war. It has grown in terms of ground coverage. The centre hasn't changed a great deal, the Pavilion, the last big change, was fifty years ago.

The De La Warr Pavilion was built by Rice and Co., from Brighton, and the contract figure was £80,000. It was just over the road for us so it was a great event. I saw it growing every day and I saw them pulling down the old coastguard cottages which occupied the site. That was great. They had this big old steam roller, anchored a steel piece on the back end of the houses, threw it over the roof and hooked it on the steam roller and off it chuntered and it just cut the houses like cutting cheese with a wire. Most exciting and I really enjoyed that. The building was one of the first welded steel frame buildings and it was fascinating. Fascinating watching this and we were proud of it because it was really quite something and Bexhill was doing this.

I remember it very well. I was about 15. My parents were in favour. There was a lot of discussion but I think most everybody felt that the entertainment hall, as it was called, would be a great addition and I suppose in a funny kind of way Bexhill was one of the last in the field again. Hastings and Eastbourne had their theatres and so Bexhill finally got around just in time for the English seaside holiday to disappear, so the Pavilion came after it was wanted in a way, but it has still been a great asset to the town.

I was delighted when it was built. I was a young man. This building is terrific as far as I'm concerned, it was a source of great pride. It's always been terrific I don't remember any kind of sense of shock at the design from people of my father's generation. In fact all Bexhill seemed to like it and my parents were much in favour and very pleased to be able to walk in after it had been done.

The theatre was quite well used before the war, there were Sunday evening variety shows which I went to as a young lad. They had quite big events; Paul Robeson came and sang on one occasion and people like Arthur Askey in his early days and Dickie Murdoch. It really wasn't used like it is today. The Elizabeth Room was a reference library and the Edinburgh Room was a meeting room. The theatre bar wasn't used as a bar and the bottom part was a little restaurant, but it was more like a seaside tea room.

Deck games. De La Warr Pavilion.

There may have been a dance band in the long restaurant. I remember the Elizabeth Room; it wasn't elegant, it was low ceilinged and it had those three stanchions up the middle but they were lost in the library bookshelves and they didn't stick out like a sore thumb like they do today. It wasn't elegant, it was functional.

The thing I miss now compared with it then was the use of the roof. That was absolutely marvellous. We used to play deck quoits up there. I was a boy of 15. They didn't have building regulations in those days and it wasn't dangerous, yes, young people went up there. People behaved themselves when I was a boy.

Community life; I've played a part to a large extent. I joined the Round Table, formed in 1948, subsequently Rotary.

I think in some ways there is a stronger community spirit at this time now than there was before the war. We were still a segregated community in a way. There were the Brasseys, Sackvilles, De La Warrs and slightly lower down the Sewells. The kind of aristocracy of the town, and then a middle class. But that has all disappeared and there is a better spirit now I think.

Bexhill is a funny place. As I see it there is an indigenous population which has a social life like a family. Imposed on that there are different people who only come here when they are retiring, and I say nothing against them, but they are not part of the social structure of the town. They are almost like its bread and butter.

There was not such a strong retirement element before the war. The town relied very strongly on independent schools and the seaside holiday for economic survival but it was the schools really. We didn't see ourselves as a retirement town but a holiday and schools town. Some of the older people who came to town were ex-Indian Army and you could see that lovely map of the world with the pink blobs on it*. They were really empire people when they congregated in the Bexhill Club and the Constitutional Club.

I regret Bexhill losing town status. I say nothing against Rother or our council but I think it was a great sadness when we lost municipal borough status. The mayor was held in very high esteem in those days and to me at least it was a tragedy and I don't think it has been good for Bexhill. The De La Warr family had influence but were not dominant.

---

* The British Empire was shown coloured pink on world maps

Footnote: *Sadly Peter Evenden died a short while before this book was published. When he was interviewed he revealed a special knowledge of the town and a particular affection for the De La Warr Pavilion which he saw built. This led to his part in the founding of the Pavilion Trust. The knowledge, vision and support he gave to the Trust was mirrored with many organisations throughout Bexhill.*

# William Gordon Harris born 1918

I was born on 2nd May 1918. I had three older sisters, Marjorie, Rene and Doreen who was nicknamed 'Bunty', she was just a little over a year older than me. At that time we were living at 24, Station Road, opposite the Central Station Goods Yard (now Sainsbury's car park) and we were often woken in the morning by the lowing of the cows awaiting transportation.

Our parents, William Gordon Harris and mother, Florence Douthy, came to Bexhill in the 1890s. Father was from Woolwich where my grandfather was a builder. William and his younger brother Charley got on their bicycles and came to the South Coast looking for work; they first went to Hastings, but Bexhill was growing then and they decided to stay, taking 'digs' in Reginald Road. They set up a small lock-up shop in Station Road, (but on the opposite side of the road to where we lived). Subsequently they had a shop in St. Leonards Road. They advertised for work as painters and decorators and sought work in the town. That's how my parents met.

The shop of W. Gordon Harris decorated for the triumphant return of Earl De La Warr from the Boer War.

Mother was running a shoe shop at that time. She had at one time lodged with a Station Master and his wife at Bromley. They were childless and when Mr Minor retired he offered to set up mother, (she had originally trained as a seamstress) in the newly developing town of Bexhill. He became her delivery boy and rode around the town on a large heavy bike taking samples of shoes to the many independent boarding schools in the area; the matrons were responsible for ordering a selection of shoes as required by the pupils.

Father and Uncle Charley were joined in their business by Uncle Thomas. Their workshop was in the mews behind Caffyns and their yard in Buckhurst Road, near where the roller skating rink had been. During the 1914-18 war Canadian soldiers used the building as a barracks; once Bunty, who was only about two, took herself off for a walk and got as far as Devonshire Road. Fortunately one of the Canadians recognised her and brought her home on his shoulders; of course I don't remember this.

A builders yard makes an exciting playground, it was surrounded by a ten foot wall with brick piers between. We had a Club there called the 'Daring Cowboy Club' and in order to join you had to jump off the wall. I was Tom Mix* and Bunty (who was a great tomboy) called herself Bob Tom Mix. Bunty liked to dress up in my old trousers, and once when our parents went on holiday to Belgium they brought us each back a knitted trouser suit.

My sisters attended St. Josephs School in Buckhurst Road and I was very sad when Bunty went off without me but she said 'we could still be friends'. On her first day there I went up with my little go-cart and sat outside waiting for her to come out so I could take her home in it. Mother was a good sport, once I took her for a ride in it from behind Station Road to father's yard. The cart was made from a Tate and Lyle sugar box, it was a double-decker. We used to take it to the top of Buckhurst Road and then race it down the hill, to the Town Hall Square. There were only horses about, so we were in no danger but the police stopped us.

*Tom Mix was a film star cowboy, popular in the 1920s.

Mr. and Mrs. Gordon Harris and their family in 1922.

I had a particular friend, Dick Gouldsmith, who lived at 6, Amherst Road. He and I were interested in electricity, so we wanted to fix up a wire between our houses. I got the wire onto the ridge of the roof and then tied it onto the fence of the allotments in Buckhurst Road. We intended to join the two ends above the wall and tighten it up after dark, but unfortunately Dick's grandfather discovered it and wound it up. Dick had got his section over the entrance to the Conservative Club so we only had to cross Buckhurst Road to make a complete circuit. We were both very disappointed as we had hoped to pass messages in morse down the wire.

I was first introduced into the mysteries of wireless sets in the early 1930s when I was about 11 years old, after I met an elderly gentleman who only had simple crystal sets. He had no electricity in his house and his only illumination was from oil lamps. The components consisted of a hand wound coil, a variable condenser, and cat's whisker mounted in a short glass tube. He would turn up the wick of his lamp which would show up the bright spots on his crystal on which he would adjust his cat's whisker. We then held our breath and loud and clear we could hear Radio Fecamp and at a lower volume we could pick up Luxemburg and under good conditions Radio Paris and Daventry. I then made a number of crystal sets which were highly successful.

I still have my crystal and cat's whisker and without success I have tried to interest my young grandsons who are more interested in having a modern transistor radio!!

My father then supported me by ordering *Practical Wireless* each week instead of *Comic Cuts* and I then moved on to a battery operated valve set. My income was thruppence a week pocket money and therefore it restricted my experiments. I scrounged anything I could lay my hands on, including worn out valves. I acquired an accumulator, which needed charging from time to time, for the low tension. Our house was wired for d.c. so I cut the main cable between the meter and the house fuses, inserted a two-way switch so that I could connect my accumulator in series to act as a charger through the lighting system. I then offered to charge my friend's batteries and, having several in series, my father could not understand why the lights in his house were so dim, he blamed the local electricity generating station!

I obtained an old ignition coil from a Model 'T' Ford, which I put to use when a transformer burnt out; I would connect the high tension leads across the defective windings which created a spark across the burnt out winding, which had the effect of either welding or shorting out the defective break. However, it usually seemed to work.

I then decided to try to transmit in morse to my friend who lived nearby. As a first stage I connected the output of my Ford coil to my aerial and to earth. My experiment was short-lived as I heard that neighbours in the area were complaining of intense interference on their wireless sets which coincided with my broadcasts.

*Practical Wireless* at one time included a series of competitions on common radio faults, inviting readers to write in with solutions. One issue included the following problem, 'When I switch on my radio (or should I say "wireless"!) it works perfectly well for a short period and then becomes very faint. What is the fault?' I wrote in to say the battery was running down. To my surprise I received an edition of Newnes

*Wireless Constructors Encyclopaedia* by F.J. Camm as a prize. This included details on building a television set.

William Gordon Harris aged 13, at the time he built his first television set.

I was then about 13 years old and I set off to purchase from a car breaker an aluminium door panel from which I cut a 22 inch scanning disc and punched thirty holes, each 1/30th of an inch, in a spiral. This I then mounted on an old electric motor. A neon bulb (robbed from a night light) was connected into the out-put of my wireless.

In those days television was broadcast once a week at 11pm for half an hour from London Regional for testing purposes. Subject to preparing for bed and being in my pyjamas my mother allowed me to stay up for the half hour broadcast. To make the thing work it was necessary to spin the scanning disc at the rate of 750 revolutions a minute. I had no variable resistance to control the speed so I improvised using a jam jar of water having two electrodes. To increase the speed I added two or three pinches of salt and to reduce the speed I pulled the electrodes apart. Looking back it was a wonder I did not electrocute myself with all the water swilling around.

The idea was to tune in the wireless to full power, disconnect the loudspeaker and connect the neon bulb which started to glow and fluctuate with the signal.

By 10.55 p.m. I was in business, and my jar of water, salt cellar and disc spinning at high speed. My parents and three sisters came up to my room to enjoy their first television programme. The picture was about one inch square and when they had fought for a front seat I hardly had a look-in what with having to adjust the quantity of salt. I cannot say that I ever saw a picture because we were all so tense with excitement, pushing and shoving, that we could have imagined seeing anything. My mother was certain that she had seen a fleeting picture, and always maintained that she really had, but I wonder whether she was just being kind to me after my efforts!!

We had a car, it was a Morris Cowley. I had priority and sat on mother's lap in the front while the three girls sat in the back. We often went for picnics. When I was bigger father installed a stool for the younger children to sit on.

We attended the Congregational Church, the three girls were dressed in navy-blue princess line dresses with red leather belts, white collars with a red bow, woollen stockings and red Charleston' sandals. I was not very keen on church and used to smuggle in my homework and do that. After church we always went for a walk on the sea front. We swam from Buxton's sea bathing station and sometimes took our tea there for a picnic on the beach.

The girls joined the Guides and later I joined the Scouts. Bunty always carried the banner in the procession to the War Memorial on November 11th. One year we camped in the school playing fields.

I first started school at St. Josephs but when I was eight my father sent me to St. Barnabas School for boys in Reginald Road, as, being the only boy, he wanted to toughen me up.

My two older sisters were first-day pupils at the newly built County Secondary (subsequently Grammar) school and I followed them there. I was never very academic but I enjoyed using my hands and my father had given me a workshop of my own when I was quite young. At school I enjoyed work in the woodwork shop and demonstrated special lathe work one Speech Day.

We were not allowed to mix with the girls in the adjoining school. Miss Davis, the girls headmistress, was very strict but Mr Lamb was far more tolerant. We sometimes climbed into the roof space and spied on the girls working in the laboratories, but one day one of the boys slipped on the rafters and his leg went through the ceiling but he managed to pull himself up. The caretaker told the headmaster that he thought it was broken due to expansion of rafters and cracked asbestos sheets, but we believe Mr Lamb knew how it had happened.

Miss Davis wouldn't allow brothers and sisters to walk home together. One day she (or it could have been her deputy Miss Poole) caught me giving Bunty a ride home on my crossbar. Miss Davis wrote a complaint to my father, but he wrote back to her, 'that I have no objection to my daughter walking home with her brother and that is how it is going to be.' Miss Davis requested that Bunty be removed for not wearing her panama hat and breaking rules. She said, 'you are always misbehaving, always causing trouble and climbing on the roof retrieving balls.' However, Bunty continued to remain at school.

Upper Sea Road earlier this century

We moved from 24, Station Road to 22, Station Road and then when I was in my teens we went to 'Marendor' (called after my sisters' names) in Upper Sea Road. It is quite a coincidence that John Logie Baird lived from 1942 until his death in 1946 a few doors away on the opposite side of the road.

Father had been instrumental in getting up a petition to build a footbridge over the railway from Station Road to Devonshire Square. Father was never a good timekeeper and once had to send my two older sisters to the station to ask them to hold the London train for him.

Like most children of our generation we led a fairly simple life. Mother enjoyed tennis and played in Egerton Park. I used to cycle to Eastbourne on the old road and often we went blackberrying. Father tied a ladder on the side of the car so that we could reach the ones growing higher up the hedges. Other drives we took in the car were to Rye and Camber and father gave us 1d to open the many gates through which we passed. Once I went on a 5/- flight when Alan Cobham's Flying circus came to the recreation ground in Little Common. I must have been 14 or 15 then.

I left school at 17 and started to train with John Bray & Sons of St. Leonards. Father paid a premium of £100 and I was given 5/- a week. Commander Bray said that if I studied with a postal course (as well as my office training) he would raise my wages to 15/- a week. This enabled me to run a motor bike. My Articles finished just before World War II broke out. As I had joined the RNVR I was called up on 28th August, 1939.

I returned to Brays after the war and the wages offered to me were then £2 a week. I could not afford to live on that as I was getting married and decided against rejoining the firm but instead joined the Valuers Office of the Inland Revenue at Guildford where the salary was £8 a week. I qualified as a Chartered Auctioneer in 1948. Subsequently the Chartered Auctioneers amalgamated with the Chartered Surveyors. For a time I worked at Reigate but decided to return to Bexhill and bought a partnership in Riches & Gray. The immediate post-war business was very slow especially as it was the policy of the firm not to advertise. The first property I sold in Bexhill went for £500.

William Gordon Harris c.1943.

Footnote: *William Gordon Harris served on battle cruisers escorting fast merchantmen carrying Canadian troops across the Atlantic during the early part of the war. He was also on HMS Hood prior to her sinking by the Bismark in 1941. Subsequently he went on the Russian convoys, on one occasion only three of the 27 merchant ships arrived at their final destination, due to enemy action. Finally he went to the Far East in Combined operations, leaving the Navy in 1946.*

# Mollie Hickie née Willing born 1914

I was born in Little Common on August 16th 1914, brought into the world by Dr. Stokes at my grandmother's house, 'Brentwood', in Cooden Sea Road. The Great War having just begun and my father, Frederick Willing, expected to be called up at any minute. Awaiting my birth he paced up and down in front of the house wearing his uniform, presumably from the Boer War. But, as an employee of the Bank of British West Africa it was decided otherwise by the authorities and he returned to the Gold Coast the next day. When my mother joined him there I was left in the care of my grandmother and young twin aunts.

I think the house was rented from Colonel Webb of 'The Pages'. I remember being taken in my pram or push-chair up the long tree-lined drive to his house. On the way there we would have passed the big mirror on that sharp bend in Collington Lane [West], it was always a thrill to see one's-self in there! Another entertainment was shouting loudly under the cattle arch and hearing the echo.

Perhaps because my mother stayed in Little Common after the birth of my brother in 1916, not being allowed to travel back to West Africa at that stage of the war, and I had undoubtedly been spoilt by Granny and the aunts, I was jealous of Peter and was told that on one occasion I bit him. I distinctly remember being so resentful at being made to lend him my beloved golliwog to take out in his pram that I removed Golly's jacket so at least he shouldn't have that! Fate decreed that I should be punished for my selfishness, as during the walk, when apparently I was not present, Golly was thrown out of the pram and lost.

One of my aunts taught music at Seafield School, and I remember being taken to the Sports Day there and spending my time rolling down a grassy bank. When younger still I remember standing on tip-toe to see the ice on the water-trough outside the school.

All I remember of the Great War is seeing the convalescent soldiers in their bright blue suits and red ties, and a map in the hall with little flags on it. At the end of the war there must have been some sort of parade through the village. I was given a small Union Jack and told to go to the gate and wave it to the soldiers marching past.

Mrs. Willing with her two children, Mollie and Peter in 1917.

The ice on the horse-trough was the last I saw for about six years, as, when I was five we went to live in Egypt, my father having been transferred to Alexandria as General Manager of the branch there. We always came back to Little Common on leave while my grandmother was alive and I imagine my memories of the shops date mostly from those times.

We enjoyed going to Mr. Duke's for groceries and watching him make clever little blue bags for sugar etc. I remember his cheerful face and rosy cheeks well. The Misses Coad at the Post Office were kind and friendly too, as was Mrs. Saunders at the Bakery next door. Mr. Saunders was seldom seen, I expect he was busy baking.

There was a big tree in the middle of the Common, where we sat and watched for the little blue bus that took us into Bexhill. I remember seeing the wagons piled high with hay or corn passing through the village, and being so envious of some small children riding on the top of one. The nearest I ever came to doing anything like that was standing on the top of a hayrick I'd helped to build during the last war.

Little Common Village

Mollie Hickie and her grandmother with her father home on leave from Africa in August 1916. The houses seen in the background are in Churchhill Avenue.

When I was ten I was sent to Little St. John's in Collington Avenue. This building still stands, it is a rest-home now and two bungalows are built on the greater part of the garden where we used to play and have our own small plots.

The senior school, St. John's and annexe, St. John's Lodge, were both demolished when Thrift House (now re-named Conquest House and occupied by Hastings Direct) was built on the site. I happened to be walking past during the demolition work and watched a bulldozer scooping up the remains of the Lodge dining-room.

St. John's School from the air showing the 21 tennis courts,. The grounds covered an area from Collington Avenue to Cranston Avenue.

St. John's was founded in 1820, and was unique in that it was carried on, from then until it closed in 1940, by three generations of the same family. Started in Bermondsey, the school moved to Reigate, Exeter and Brighton before coming to Eversley Road in 1903. In 1910 the school moved into the large purpose-built house in Collington Avenue, and two years later Miss E.B. Hamilton, who had recently taken over from her mother as principal, bought the adjacent building, The Lodge. There were places for 120 boarders in all, 20 of whom were in the Little House, as we called it. By my time day girls were no longer accepted. Hockey and netball were played in Autumn and Spring terms and in summer, tennis on the 21 courts.

St. John's was a splendid school and I thoroughly enjoyed my six years and a term there, and still have many good friends made there. In retrospect it was very old fashioned, and the regime very strict, even for those days. The clothes-list was very long, almost everything 'regulation' and to be bought from Gorringes. In summer when we were wearing short-sleeved dresses, we had to wear long gloves to the elbow, brown to match everyday dresses and white ones on Sundays. We went to church at St. Mark's, walking in crocodile all the way of course. We went up Collington Rise, known to us as the 'Cinderpath'. There were not many houses then, and still woods on one side of the road most of the way. After church and a short break, we set forth again for what for us was known as 'The advertisement walk', when all 120 of us, escorted by Miss 'Ham' as we called her, and a member of the staff, went over Collington Halt footbridge and down Richmond Road to parade along the front as far as the Colonnade, where we turned, and retraced our steps back to school for lunch.

Mollie Hickie, a pupil at Little St. John's spent her holidays with her aunt, Jo Birnie. c.1925.

No-one left school at half-term or any other weekend in those days; parents came and took us out for the day on Saturday and Sunday, after church. The parents stayed mainly at the Sackville Hotel, a few at the Granville or Normanhurst. We were told not to let our parents take us down Western Road, in case we caught germs from the school at the corner, now the Library. Removing one's gloves, hats, or eating sweets or ice creams in the street were also forbidden, likewise going to cinemas.

We were allowed to buy sweets once a week from Mrs. Roberts, who brought a selection from her shop in Collington Mansions. One shilling and sixpence (7½p) was the maximum one was allowed to spend, and all had to be consumed during free time on Saturday and Sunday. Anything left over was taken into safe keeping until the following week. On the School's birthday and a few other special occasions the shops 'came up,' and had stalls in the gym where we could buy stationery and haberdashery etc. This was a great excitement.

We also enjoyed picnics in Collington Woods. We were each given a 'nose-bag', a white paper bag containing a hard-boiled egg, some lettuce leaves, a meat pie, a bun and an apple or banana. The meat pies we called 'Pook's Porky Puffs', I have no idea why.

In November the Little Common Bonfire Boys paid us a visit and we also had a splendid firework display every year while the Brock girls were at St. John's.

We often had cinema shows on Saturday evenings in the gym, listened to the Boat-race on the wireless, and had apple-bobbing and obviously got wet on All Hallow's Eve.

Morning and Evening prayers also took place in the gym every day and hymn singing every Sunday evening.

Every morning when the maid came into our bedroom to wake us and bring hot water for the wash stands, she was greeted with, 'Good morning Sophie, what's for breakfast today?' Kippers were very unpopular and groans went up from most beds. Sausage rolls were very popular and expressions of delight came from all directions.

The Gymnasium at St. John's School. c.1920.

When I first went to Little St. John's we had a most unusual type of matron there, most unlike any other we had and I do not think she lasted very long. When asked why I did not kneel down by my bed to say my prayers I informed her that at home (in Egypt) I always said my prayers in bed 'because of the fleas on the floor'. This statement, together with the fact that I was provided with a sponge and loofah, but no face-flannel, prompted her to call me 'a dirty little foreigner'. Later she shocked me by washing the spoon in my bath-water after giving me the regulation Friday evening dose of Syrup of Figs and then going on to my friend in the next door bathroom. And, as she had told us that she only washed her hair once a year it occurred to me even then that she was not particularly clean!

In Summer we went, in crocodile of course, to the Swimming Baths in Egerton Park. On hot summer days we had to take our umbrellas to use as parasols. A very Scottish Matron used to tell us when we came out to 'Put up your gamps'. Aged ten and straight from Egypt this was quite incomprehensible to me and I just stood and gaped until I realised that I was the only one without an open umbrella.

St. John's School far left, The Annexe and Little St. John's in Collington Avenue. c. 1930.

I enjoyed school so much, always being glad to go back every term and see my friends again, that the thought of leaving filled me with sorrow so much that I cried myself to sleep on the eve of my 16th birthday in the realisation that I only had one more year left at school. I had no wish to be 'grown-up'.

After I left in 1931 I trained to be a Kennel-Maid at Dollmead Kennels, Haslemere, and a couple of years later returned to Bexhill to work for a short time for Miss Arnold, who ran a small boarding kennel at her cottage opposite the Cooden Beach Hotel. An old coastguard cottage, it was demolished when Westbourne Court flats were built. When Earl De La Warr and his family came to stay at his hotel, the nurse and children had my room and a room was found for me elsewhere.

My parents had left Egypt and were living in Suffolk by this time, but one of my twin aunts was living in Bexhill and I spent all my free time with her. After my job with Miss Arnold came to an end I decided I would prefer drawing dogs to being a kennel-maid. So in order to go to the Vita Studio in Manor Road I went as an 'au pair' to a rather peculiar

Western Road earlier in the century.

lady in Jameson Road. My duties were to help her and go about with the foreign students she took-in during the Summer. During the morning, while she gave them lessons, I attended the Studio. She used to shop in Western Road on Saturday evenings to get things more cheaply. One day she produced a chicken for Sunday lunch which turned out to be full of maggots. Undeterred she scooped them out and put it in the oven. Oddly enough no-one was ill after eating it! I had a good time with the students, French, Spanish, Swedish and German. Once a German boy burnt a French lady's newspaper on the beach because it said something derogatory about Hitler. It was not much fun being alone with her in the winter. Once she announced that she hated all men except King George V and one Frenchman.

The Augusta Victoria College from the north-side in Dorset Road, now the site of the 'Seafield Nursing Home.'

Miss Hoskin, who owned the Vita Studio and was in every way most kind and helpful to me, told me that the Augusta-Victoria College in Dorset Road was always wanting English au-pairs to be with the German girls who were studying for the Cambridge Certificate of Proficiency in English. So just after my 21st birthday I went to live at the College (now Seafield Lodge Nursing Home). My parents came to live in Cranston Rise not long after this, and my brother worked in the Devonshire Road Branch of Lloyds Bank for a short time before joining the R.A.F.

I was very happy at the College and made a lot of good friends. At one time I shared a room with Bettina von Ribbentrop (daughter of the German Ambassador to Britain at the time) and another girl who was a god-daughter of Himmler. A Princess Herzeleide was at the College for a short time. She was engaged to a grandson of the Kaiser, and, when she went up to London to meet him for the day she borrowed clothes from various friends as she thought none of her own were smart enough.

I often went to Germany during this time and once to Finland to stay with a Finnish girl with whom I'd been friendly during her year at the College. Just before the outbreak of World War II I was in Austria with my German fiancé (brother of one of the girls who had been at the College), it was August 1939 and I was due to return to Bexhill at the end of the month. Although I was tempted to stay I set out on the journey home. I had to change trains in Aachen and had some time there. I spent it visiting the police and registry offices, enquiring what would happen to me if there was a war, and if I could get married at once. I forgot what they said at the registry office, but the police said 'we wouldn't do anything to pretty young girls.' I returned to the station telling myself if I'd missed the train I'd go back to Salzburg. But I caught it, and went on as far as Brussels, where I changed my mind, got out and took a taxi to the German Embassy. It was Saturday and a woman cleaning the Embassy steps told me that everyone was away and wouldn't be back till Monday. Unable to face the thought of a weekend alone and with not much money left, back I went to the station and took the next train to Ostend. Having, of course, missed my boat I had to wait 'till evening for the next. I spent the time sitting on the beach in tears.

The crossing took longer than usual, the boat zigzagging about. I thought this rather strange, and learnt later that mines had already been laid in the Channel. I got as far as Ashford on the Sunday morning and was told there was a very long time before there would be a train to Bexhill, so I phoned my father, who was no doubt vastly relieved to know that I was back in England and drove over to bring me home to Cranston Rise in time for lunch. By this time all the staff and girls from the College had gone back to Germany, so I lived at home and went to the Studio again regularly until it closed.

I worked as a telephonist in the A.R.P. Centre in Amherst Road until it was decided that it was not safe to have someone with a German fiancé there and I was asked to leave.

Mollie Hickie in the WRNS c.1945

**Footnote:** *After Dunkirk when invasion seemed imminent all persons not involved in essential occupations were asked to leave Bexhill. Mollie and her mother were among these people. For some years during the war Mollie worked on the land; the Police continued to keep an eye' on her and her employers were asked if they knew about her past. Mollie joined the WRNS in 1943, her brother Peter was shot down on a bombing raid over the coast of Eritrea and her fiancé was killed on the Russian front. In December 1945, still a Wren, Mollie was sent to Germany. She met her future husband, ex RNVR, in Hamburg and they were married there in 1947. After several years in Germany and ten in West Africa and many visits to Bexhill over the years they eventually returned here.*

# Ted Hollands born 1919

Edward Victor Hollands, born 24 November 1919 in Reginald Road, Bexhill. Five brothers and one sister. I was the last but one to be born.

My father was a builder on the building all his life. He was born in All Saints Street, Hastings. He came to live in Bexhill in the early 1900s, I think.

My mother was born in Catford, Lewisham. I don't know how they met. Parents never spoke much about their private lives when you was children, it's funny isn't it? Now I've told all my two boys and a girl everything, how Betty and I met and they think it's wonderful, but your parents weren't prepared to; 'Oh we haven't got time to waste talking about things like that.' And you never got to know. Shame isn't it?

We lived in Reginald Road, terrace houses, some had two stories and some had three stories. They were all built by different builders.

We had to rent ours. My mother and father never owned a house, worse luck, the rent was thirteen shillings. I can tell you the reason why I remember. When we used to get bad winters and there was no work for my father to do they had to go on the dole. Well in those days you had to sign on for nine days before you were even allowed to get any money and then you only got three days. The dole money was about 17s 6d a week, it didn't even come to pay the rent. Well, it didn't make any difference how many children you had. There was a Means Test. If you were in difficulties you used to go to the British Legion. They used to give you a food voucher. And also there was a Relief Officer, Mr. Cane, he lived in Colebroooke Road. You went and saw him and he gave you a voucher say for ten shillings worth of groceries and a voucher for a sack of coal. My father used to hate doing that. Well if we got bad winters, you know, 'cos there was no guarantee of a wage, you just hoped for the best, that the weather would turn better and you could get back to work. 'Cos there was always work, you know, in the building trade but if the weather was bad you got sent home and that was it.

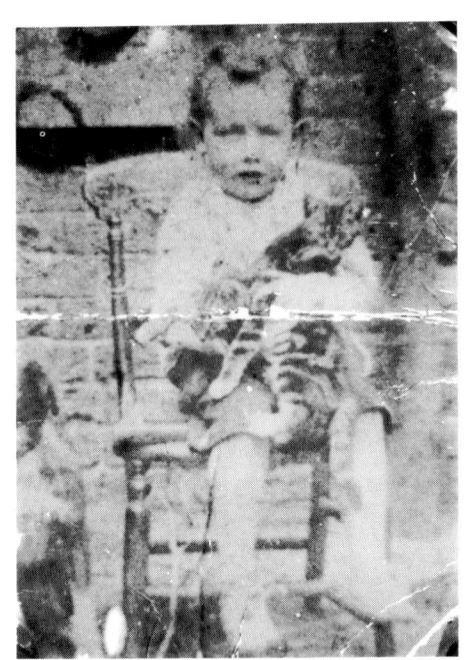

Ted Holland aged two

Illness, I'll tell you what happened. Now when my mother paid her rent each week, she paid 3d a week in the Hospital Fund for each one of us that was living at home, which was Alf, myself, Dick and Tom, and a shilling a year for each one of us for an ambulance. When she was taken ill in 1947 and they took her to the R.E.S.H. and I got a bill for £5, that was the year before the Health Service started, I went and queried it 'cos the man who used to collect our rents worked for a House Agent called Burstow and Hewitt in Town Hall Square. I went and saw him and said, 'Look we can't pay this, we haven't got £5'. 'Oh no,' he says, 'you belong to the Ambulance Fund.' 'That's right', I said, 'my mother pays 1s each for all four of us and 3d a week so if anyone is ill and we have to go into hospital that 3d pays for it.' And my mother did that for years, even if it meant going without something else she made sure that one shilling a week was paid for us four boys. I think it used to be well half a crown if you wanted to go and see a doctor in those days when I was a lad. But if you belonged to this, 3d a week, that covered it. So it was good, wasn't it? My mother made sure that that was paid every week, and that would have been £5 for the ambulance that year.

I attended St. Barnabas Infants school, where the library now stands, for boys and girls. Oh lovely classrooms. Always nice and warm as far as I can remember, they used to have open fires. Oh lovely it was. I know one thing, I could read and write and do all my sums before I left there, in one year. We sat in desks there'd be like a boy and a girl, a boy and a girl, and you couldn't look over one another's shoulders. The headmistress was Miss Matthews, my teacher was Miss Evans, she used to bring toys from Woolworths, so it gave you incentives to learn quickly. Prizes at the end of each week on a Friday afternoon just before we broke up for the week-end. It was like a little crane or a little motor car and you didn't know what you were going to get it for, it might be penmanship or spelling or knowing all your tables. It was a good system, she was a marvellous person. And it was many, many years after the war when I was a postman and I knocked on her door in Terminus Avenue. And she answered the door and she said, 'Good heavens!' She knew me straight away and I said, 'You're Miss Evans.' 'No' she said, 'Mrs. Defoy now, Mrs. Defoy.'

When I was six years of age I then attended St Barnabas School for boys in Reginald Road where Chandlers the printers are now operating. Our Headmaster was "Caley", Mr Poulton, a wonderful man. Then there was Mr Rees, Mr Robins, Mr Frisby our sports master, also a real gentleman, then Mr Tommy Mitchell who had red hair and a fiery temper, who doled out the cane quite often. Anyway it did not do us any harm, if we told our mum and dad we had the cane, the reply was, 'You probably deserved it.'

I can always remember there was a blacksmith up in the Old Town. One day I wandered off from home. And they could not find me and eventually they found me up by the blacksmith and they'd rung up the local policeman and he said, 'Your little lad's up here.' Now I was only four at the time. And I'd gone up Victoria Road and round Town Hall Square, up Buckhurst Road and up Sea Road. But in those days there wasn't the cars about, I mean, that would be in 1923.

We always had lots of horses from the goods yard delivering coal so there was always lots of manure in the streets. So we used to get horse manure, a penny a bucket. I sold it to Mrs. Clifton, she only had a little back garden, just now and again she would want some to put on her garden. Then Saturday mornings to collect our pennies to go to the cinema on Saturday afternoons, we used to go to get coke for different people on our little four-wheeler carts. My brother used to be very good at making them. Get a Tate and Lyle sugar box and put a plank along the bottom of it, two wheels in the front, two wheels at the back. Then a piece of string round the front axle. We used to wheel it down to the Gas Yard in Ashdown Road get, probably, two bags on there, take 'em back home. Then do that, probably, three times during the course of a Saturday morning to get a penny a bag. The pictures were Saturday afternoon, that was St. George's Cinema round the Town Hall Square. It used to be 4d to go in. That was the only means we could get 'cos your father couldn't afford to. Our father used to give us a penny on a Saturday lunch time. Then, I mean, if you wanted anything you had to earn it.

The Old Town Forge seen on the left. Ted Hollands walked here form his home in Reginald Road when he was only four years of age. On the right is South Lodge, now demolished. c.1930.

Up Reginald Road we all used to congregate under the lamp post and we'd play hop scotch. And we'd have our tops and big iron hoops. We used to play tag and follow the leader and the girls used to do their own skipping. The girls kept to the girls and the boys used to play leap frog, tag and marbles. We was never pushed to find something to do. We was always finding games to play. And when our parents came out and said, 'Come on! time to come in.' You just said, 'Good night lads', to Bill, Tom, Ted, Dick and you went off in. But we were very lucky we had those fields where what I call the tin shack town is now, up Terminus Road. They were fields and we used to spend our whole childhood in there. We had cricket and football. The garage down in the corner of Victoria Road what was Smith's, was Green's when I was a child, and we, well not only me, but several of us) had windows backing on this garage facing towards Terminus Road and more often than not when one of our lads took a mighty swipe at a cricket ball— Crash! there's another window! But he never sort of stopped us from playing though and we had some marvellous times down in that field. Girls, well I suppose they kept nearer to home. I don't know where they were. When I was seven or eight upwards to thirteen it was nearly all boys.

A favourite playground of the young Hollands was Collington Woods. Their father had an allotment adjoining.

My father had an allotment up by Collington Wood and Sunday mornings he would get up and cook the breakfast for all of us to give my mother a rest. And he would say, 'Come along we are going to the allotment today, get some more things, take a basket.' And we'd go up there and while he was probably busy, my brother and I would go into Collington Woods 'cos there was always something to do in there. We were sort of made to go to church. Sunday school in the morning, St.Andrews or St Barnabas (St Barnabas was the mother church). And we used to have to go on Sunday afternoons. Then come home to tea and then sit there if it was winter time read books or play with toys. In the summer evenings we'd probably go out along the sea front for a walk oh yes go swimming or do all sorts of things.

There was a place in Victoria Road, and over that was our Boy's club. We used to go up some wooden steps it was quite a big room. We used to do all sorts of learning like Cubs did, tying knots. It was always kept as a boy's club. Then after that it was sold to Hilder's, the mineral water people, then we used to go to Malet Hall down in London Road. And then after that when the Athletic Club was built we used to go there up to the outbreak of war.

When I was ten years of age I did a morning paper round for Mr Jimmy Mitchell at Collington Mansions Sub-Post Office. We had to be there at 6.30 to get our rounds ready. Then Mr. Mitchell or Mr Hoffman, his second-in -command, would then check them over for any mistakes. For this seven mornings a week I was paid the princely sum of 3s 6d a week. My delivery was the whole of Terminus Avenue plus four houses in Westcourt Drive, they were the only four built then, when I was a boy. Well then when I was eighteen Mr. Hart in Windsor Road said he would give me 5s if I was to do his paper round which included Windsor Road, Reginald Road and Leopold Road and it was nearer, so when I was eighteen I transferred my affections and did that till I was called up. I still did a paper round even when I carried on at Boots the Chemists 'cos I didn't have to start work till half past eight, the paper round used to start at half past six and used to finish at half past seven. So it gave me plenty of time to go home and have my breakfast and still get to work.

Three mornings a week an elder brother and me, armed with two pillow slips, would go to Arscott's in St Leonards Road; this was after I had done my paper round. There, there would be a queue of a dozen boys or more. My brother would get sixpenny worth of stale bread I would get sixpenny worth of stale cake. These bread and cakes were left over from the day before. I don't know what we would have done if it had not been for Mr Arscott, bless him.

I did not quite make the necessary marks required in the scolarship exam so I left school at 14. The four lads that did pass went on to the Secondary School. If I remember rightly Ted Mepham, son of the removal firm, was one of them.

When I was a boy we were set boundaries by our parents, for instance we were never to go further than Collington Wood in one direction or the Gaiety Cinema, (it stood next to the York Hotel, in London Road) in another direction. Galley Hill was one boundary and the Old Town was another. When we did go out we always had to be in by a certain time and also say where we were going so they knew where to start looking for us if we were over our time. Once or twice when we were late we had the bad luck to run into the local Bobby and he would give us a clip round the ear and tell us to get off home quick. We dare not tell our parents or we would get another roasting. The local police station was in Barrack Road. Four of the old time policemen come to mind, P.C.Biddlecombe, P.C.Butler Brown, P.C.Von de Hyde, P.C.Simmons.

After I left school it was the fashion to start life as an errand boy, which I did. I could have gone into office work for Mr Harris but that started at 5s a week and my mother said she could not afford for me to do so. While I was an errand boy I saw Bexhill grow and grow.

There was no Westville Road or Holmesdale Road when I was a small lad. Cranston Avenue had one house beyond Sutherland Avenue which was not made up till the late 30's. Where Walton Park is now stood Mayer's Wood and at the end of Cranston Avenue was a large pond which stood opposite the King Edward Memorial Home for Children, in short, Collington Manor.

Holidays were unheard of. I worked for a butcher, Mr. and Mrs. White in Collington Mansions. And then they sold up the business and went to Bournemouth. And I went to Turk's the fishmongers.

I remember being an errand boy. I had to go into Little Common for just one or two shops. Collington Lane West was full of Schools Seafield, Falconbury, Effingham, Lake House. I think there were about 25 private schools in Bexhill at one time 'cos that used to bring a lot of trade in the town. See if my memory serves me well — Winceby House, Portsdown Lodge, Collington Rise School, Mayfield, St. John's, Harewood, Thornbank, Normandale, The Beehive, Sandown, Charters Towers, Devonshire House, Ancaster House, Ancaster Gate, Wilton House, St. Mary's which was Lindore's school, Pendragon, St. Francis. Lovely schools, a lot of people even today, I bet, have got fond memories of Bexhill. So much for schools.

I can remember the trams which came from Hastings to turn around at the Metropole Hotel, now the site of the putting green. These were replaced by the trolley buses. These buses ran every 18 minutes to Hastings and the same coming back to Bexhill. The fare was sixpence single, ten pence return.

I did caddying when I was about ten. Sometimes Sunday mornings when I started going over to Bexhill Golf Club, that was Galley Hill and De La Warr Road. Oh yes there was a Golf Club and there was a caddy master well you know the Alf Evans Home, what was the printers home, now Grosvenor House. Well now all those buildings there were the Golf Club, the place where the people had their meals, the caddy master's hut where you all waited to take your turn when the professional came out to say, 'Come on I want you to carry clubs for Mr. So and So.' So you went out, see. You were paid a regular amount which was a shilling a round. Good money? Well it was and it wasn't, because sometimes you went out and you were probably about three hours going round and time you came in if you had a heavy bag to carry, you knew you'd been carrying a set of clubs. And then you might, with a bit of luck, get a sixpence tip off of the person concerned. So anyway I did that for about three years till I was about thirteen. Then I transferred my affections to Cooden because it was 1s 6d a round there and they weren't allowed to give you less than a shilling tip. That was the caddy master's orders so if anyone did give you less than a shilling you were to tell him and if that person wanted a caddy again he never got one, unless he gave a shilling tip. 'Cos the caddy master thought going round there was worth a shilling plus the 1s 6d fee.

They was all Society people at Cooden and Bexhill. Oh yes you had some very big names at Bexhill, come to play, same as at Cooden. When Lord De La Warr opened the Cooden Beach Hotel you had some very big names stayed there. A lot of them who lived in the town were members of the golf club. Then a lot used to come down, probably invited by Lord De La Warr, to stay at the hotel for the week-end because it was all good business. Also it was in easy reach of anyone living just out in the country to come by rail. You could get from London down to Cooden in an hour and a half. See, you could come down and go back again in a day. But no we used to have masses of people there. They played golf seven days a week. Sundays I'd go caddying. Saturday I was working after I left school.

Then when I was seventeen my mother wanted to go to Scotland to see her sister as they hadn't seen one another for years. So I thought the only way to earn some money was to go caddying full time, which I did on the Cooden Golf Course in 1937. And you was able to earn more money than what you could being an errand boy. You could do two or three rounds a day you see if the weather was good 'cos there was people wanting caddies in the evenings, first thing in the mornings, there was during the lunch time people would come out one o'clock and want a caddy and probably want to be back by three to play bridge or something. Then there's people want a game at 4 o'clock and people want a game before dinner at seven o'clock. You always had a chance to earn quite a bit of money in those days. Well when I was seventeen the rounds were 2s they'd be then, and the lowest tip they could give to a First Class Caddy was 1s 6d. So you could earn anything up to 9 to 10 shillings a day. I went in for a Putting Competition that year which the members all put so much away for the Caddy's Competition which was held about the end of October. Some of the Caddies played the big round of golf. Then we had our own putting course, you could go in for the putting. Well I went in for the Putting Competition and I won the First Prize of £2, I did, which was a lot of money. And they used to have a lovely big tea laid on for you. As you went in they gave you half a crown and twenty cigarettes so you know it was a thing we looked forward to every year but I only did it that one year to get enough money to go to Scotland, which I did, with my mother.

I can remember the old Bexhill Golf Course and some well known names of that time just before the 1939-45 war. There was Mr Shepherd who was coroner for Bexhill, Major Oaks, Mr. H.V. Robins, Mr. Moon, Mr. Carslake, Mr. Morant, a retired Indian Judge, Dr. and Mrs. O'Malley, Mrs. Clough Waters, whose son still lives in Cooden. Then there was Mr. Horace Holmes who lived in Sackville Lodge at the top of Galley Hill. It was 1933 I decided to go caddying at Cooden in my spare time. The Cooden Beach Hotel opened up about that time and the newly built Cooden Railway Station. I was always told that the station was built on condition that all trains had to stop there. I caddied for the late Pam Barton, Brigadier Critchley, the late Sir John Player who had his own cigarettes made specially for him. Douglas Fairbanks Senior played there in 1937. That year I won the caddies putting competition. So much for that!

It was all fields between Collington Rise and Little Common. In a stream grew the last watercress you could get for miles around. In the fields we used to go blackberrying and mushrooming. In Bexhill when I was a boy there was a Mr. Pedlar Palmer who had a tradesman's bicycle and he would go to the station to collect boxes of watercress to take round to the different greengrocers in the town.

I remember the Kursaal and the happy times my pals and I used to have playing underneath. Then there were the Roberts Marine Mansions in Devonshire Road. The Marine Court Flats in Marina. Haldane House, before it was called that, was reputed to be haunted, as was another house in Watermill Lane, the name I cannot recall, but it is still standing as far as I know. I can remember the first council houses being built in Bodle Crescent, Birch View and Buxton Drive. Some of the pals who I went to school with at that time said they were moving to Sidley and I was quite sad. Anyway they finished their schooling at St. Barnabas. A lot of them joined the Territorials. Since then Sidley has grown rapidly and is a thriving community. Pebsham I remember with a few holiday chalets which people used to get away for a few days and there were just a few houses.

The Kursaal and Parade, Bexhill-on-Sea.

We didn't have bikes in those days. If you owned a bike you was lucky. No there used to be trams, you got a tuppenny, they used to say tuppenny, working class return. If you go before 9 o'clock you went out to Cooden and then came back on that bus any time of the day for tuppence. Then they went out of fashion and the trolley buses came in so there was always plenty of transport. I mean the bus service in those days was marvellous, they used to run about every fifteen minutes wherever you wanted to go, Hastings, Cooden, Little Common.

Well I used to walk the streets with another young pal of mine, George Fleming, and we used to go cigarette card collecting and you know these little, miniature milk churns. I had one of them full of sets of cards. Kensitas used to do silk flags before the War, I had a set of them, jockeys, cricketers, footballers, butterflies, all different sets and when I came back from the War I think my father must have sold them to get a bit of cash. When I got back home I never did find them. I must have had hundreds of sets of all different things sportsmen, boats, trains, 'cos all the different cigarette firms used to do sets of fifty in those days. The taxi cab drivers you used to go round and they used to say, 'What number you want young Hollands?' And I used to say, 'I want No.10, No.20'. 'Alright we'll keep it for you.' That's how we used to spend our evenings going round. Yes, I went up to the Athletic Club for about two years till the War was coming on and I gave it up then and I never did go back to join the club, only as a social member after the war.

Bexhill has not improved. Its gone down terrible. Well I can remember the road sweepers, for instance, all had their own allotted span of roads to keep clean. They would never allow any weeds along the walls of the houses outside to grow. They would get like a little knife and clean it off and put some poison there. And they would have their own barrow and they would fill it up and they would take it to a certain spot and there would be a little sort of lorry come round later, pick it all up, take it to the tip. And those roads were swept religiously every day and you never saw Bexhill dirty in those days. My mother and the next door neighbours would help with their old bass brooms sweeping their fronts, shaking their carpets, their rugs. Everybody took a pride, people would be cleaning their windows and everything was as clean as a new pin. And now since the war ended, people, well I don't know, they just walk along and anything they got in their hand they just throw it down, don't they? They don't seem to have got any sense of responsibility towards keeping the place clean.

R.A. Larkin where he built them flats, we used to call that the Hollow, and we always said that would've been an ideal place for an indoor swimming pool. That stretch from Brockley Road to Richmond Road, all that Hollow they could have built something better than all them big blocks of flats.

It was a nice town It was a council, if anything wanted done, you just referred to the council and that was it. And it was either done or not done. But now to-day you got Rother, you got about thirty odd councillors and some of them say, 'Why should Bexhill have this if Battle can't have this or Rye can't have this?' I liked it when it was the

Bexhill West Parade. The sunken land on the right known as 'The Hollow' was a favourite playground for local children before the building of the 'West Indies' blocks of flats.

Ted Hollands.

old Borough Council back in 1969. Things got done, didn't they? I don't like these different villages and towns, its not the same as Bexhill up to the outbreak of war although, mind you, I did say to my father and mother, 'If I survive the war I'm not coming back to Bexhill.' They said, 'Why not?' I said, 'Oh its a dead god-forsaken hole. You got two cinemas. There's nothing for youngsters to do.' And the same applies to-day, doesn't it, same applies. I mean they say, 'You got the Athletic Club, you got this, you got that.' But they haven't, have they? Last of all Bexhill has grown out of all proportion. Developers are knocking down old places which is very sad.

**Footnote:** *Ted was 20 when the war started in 1939. He went into the army and trained as a cook. He saw service in North Africa and Italy. When he was demobbed he became a cook at the Cooden Beach Golf Club. Then in 1950 he became a postman and retired from the job in 1979. Since then he has spent his time gardening, playing golf and bowling.*

# Pauline Lane née Cook born 1922

I was born in Bexhill in 1922. At that time my parents lived in Barrack Road. The house still exists. It is the last in the road nearest to King Offa Way.

My father was a dentist with a practice in Hastings and Bexhill. Soon after I was born we moved to a house in Sea Road which became both his surgery and our home. 'Hillside', 25, Sea Road was a tall Edwardian house. I had one sister, Daphne, four years older than me. We also had a 'live in' maid who ushered patients in to my father as well as working for the family. My mother did all the cooking, sewing and knitting, she was very good at these skills. There was a large box in the kitchen with all the bells in the house marked on it. The maid must have had a good deal of climbing up and down the stairs during her day's work.

I started school at about five, going to kindergarten in Cantelupe Road, 'The Gables.' We used to walk up Upper Sea Road to use the playing field belonging to the senior school, now 'Linkwell' in the Old Town. There was a little flight of steps from the narrow pavement that led directly on to the field.

When I was a little older I went to Greencroft School in Hastings Road, usually we walked but sometimes we caught a bus outside the house which took us to Dorset Road and we walked from there. Our uniform at Greencroft School was lilac mauve dresses in summer white collar and tie belt in front; navy blazers with a silver and navy cord round edges; badge on pocket; silver and mauve ties; navy tunics and white blouses in winter. Then about 1935 I went to Charters Towers, we wore the brown and yellow uniform that the girls wore 'till the school closed a few years ago.

Sport was my main interest at school so that is what I remember best. I used to play tennis and hockey for the school. There were many schools to compete against in Bexhill and sometimes we played away in Hastings. Our school had a particularly fine Sports Day and we had a beautiful field for it. Like all other Bexhill schools Charters Towers was evacuated in 1940. As I was nearly eighteen I left school then.

Pupils of Charters Tower School in 1937. Pauline Lane is fourth from the left in the middle row. The girls are wearing the typical school uniform of the period, the pinafore known as 'gymslips'.

Although I was taught ballroom dancing at school we also went to dancing school and to a gymnasium. There was also an Art School for the more talented. As far as I remember these were separate institutions which were used by the schools. Our school had a swimming hut at East Parade and we used to walk down across the old Bexhill golf course, under a railway bridge to the beach. It was a very full day at school and when we got home at five there was homework to be done.

We spent a great deal of our free time on the beach in summer. I used to go ebony and we never thought of protecting our skin except for calamine afterwards if we were burnt. There was so much to amuse us in Bexhill. There was a Miss Baker who had Keep Fit classes on Sackville Lawn. There were races organised on that lawn and in the park. There were sand-castle competitions and children's entertainers on the terrace of the Pavilion. Sometimes we played deck quoits on the top deck of the Pavilion, which is now out of bounds. There was a society called the Children's Special Service Mission which set up a kind of platform of shingle with a big banner on it with the letters C.S.S.M. Someone would sit on the platform and play a harmonium. They would give out hymn sheets and crowds of us would gather round and have a great sing-song. Sometimes we would roller-skate along the promenade although the stretch across the Pavilion and main part of the town was forbidden to skaters. I remember knitting myself a red and white flared skating dress with military white toggles across the front. In fact we wore bathing costumes knitted by my mother when we were young.

There were fancy dress parties organised for charity usually at the Sackville in the large ballroom. In the winter there was often ice skating on the lake at Egerton Park. I remember Mr Buck from Buck's Garage skating with his hands clasped behind his back.

On Sunday we all went to church. We dressed in Sunday best, of course, including patent leather shoes and always wore hats. The hats were velour in winter and usually panama in summer. In the afternoon we went to a private Sunday School in Collington Avenue, there were about nine of us.

Charters Towers School, previously Worthingholm, in 1934 when the playing fields stretched from Hastings Road to Wrestwood Road

Pauline Lane née Cook, left of group on right. c.1935

We did go to the cinema sometimes, to carefully vetted films, Shirley Temple or Deanna Durbin, that sort of thing. There were four cinemas in Bexhill then.

For family Christmas we travelled by train to my Granny's house in Cambridge. All our clothes went in a trunk collected by the railway, transferred by rail to Cambridge and delivered to the house. This only took a day or two. The house was lit by gas lamps and I remember being frightened by them hissing when alight.

There was so much to do we did not feel we needed holidays. If we did go away we might go to the country to stay at farms or guest houses. Sometimes we might have a day out, perhaps go to a tea garden.

From about the age of ten I belonged to a tennis club. It was at the bottom of Dorset Road, all grass courts, more or less on the site of St. Richards' playing fields. In fact you can still see a little bungalow near the school which was our club house. County matches were played there and even Dan Maskell and Fred Perry have played on those courts. We girls wore white skirts and blouses.

When the war came and my school was evacuated I taught for a short time at a little school in Buckhurst Road until I went into the WAAF. Bexhill during the war had many troops stationed here. There were dances at the Metropole and the Sackville to which everyone went. There were also regular dances for the forces in the basement of what is now the RAFA Club. I enjoyed all that. At one time we evacuated ourselves to Cambridge but not for long. We came back to a house partly damaged by bombs. I remember sitting sunbathing in the garden at the time of Dunkirk and seeing a great black cloud of smoke covering the sky drifting down Channel. There was barbed wire on the beaches and the town was eerily empty for long periods. The gasholders were bombed at Glyne Gap. Bexhill as I had known it would never be the same again.

Footnote: *After service in the WAAF and marriage, Pauline and her husband finally returned to Cooden in 1995. She is still an active playing member of two tennis clubs in the town.*

# Peter Longley born 1915

In October 1906, my parents Mr. and Mrs. Walter Longley were married in Leamington Spa, and came to Bexhill to start a drapery and dressmaking business. They rented a shop at 59, Devonshire Road and opened it on 3rd. November. During the first week their takings were £26.6s.8d. as shown in their cash book.

For a short time they were assisted by my uncle, but he soon after opened a drapery business in Fleet, Hampshire. Hence the name Longley Brothers which was adopted by both firms.

Bexhill in 1906 was just beginning to recover from a period of depression after its big development boom in the 1890s, and trade was on the upgrade, fortunately on the dressmaking side where Edith Longley (née Nye) soon had a large staff in her work-room, making-up for wives and daughters of the considerable number of retired Colonial and service people who were coming to live in the town. A bill-head for 1913 advertised that the shop would provide 'Indian and Colonial Outfits' and mourning attire for both 'family' and 'complementary' wear.

The subsequent history of the firm was a story of steady and consistent expansion under the same family ownership and management. The first shop at No. 59 was ultimately surrounded by six other properties.

The firm traded through World War Two without a break despite the wholesale evacuation of Bexhill and a German bomb which in 1942 completely demolished Nos.53, 55 and 57, subsequently rebuilt in 1950. It was the end of an era in Devonshire Road when Longley Bros. department store closed for the last time in January 1985. Generations of Bexhillians had shopped there and many residents could not imagine life without Longleys!

Frances Edith, or 'Edie' as she was known, and her friend Annette Potts were both trained dressmakers and in their early twenties had travelled quite adventurously around the country by rail. When separated by reason of work Edie wrote many postcards to her friend, especially during 1904 (a number of which have survived to this day); in one she

Longley Bros. store c.1925, one of the most successful of those trading in Bexhill-on-Sea. With its closure ended an era, mourned by many.

referred to 'Mr. L.', he, of course, was Walter Longley whom she subsequently married. Annette Potts, known to the Longley children as 'Auntie Nettie' joined them in Bexhill and lived with the family until her death in the 1940s. After their marriage my parents lived in Sutherland Avenue, at the end near Collington Halt station. The road was pretty well built-up at this time. They had one child, my sister Joan, who was seven years older than me. During World War One they moved to a flat (for about three years) above the shop in Devonshire road, where I was born in 1915.

In 1917 my family moved to 'West Leigh' which was a large house towards the upper end of Sutherland Avenue. (Today a block of flats stands on the site). We had, on the ground floor, a dining room in which we had a 3/4 size billiard table, this would swing over to make a normal table. There was a hall, a drawing room which went out into a conservatory, a huge kitchen, scullery and pantry with a porch at the back, there was also a coal cellar. When wet we usually played in the dining room and our governess used to teach us there. Mother had a bell-push under her chair, it rang in the kitchen and she used to press it with her foot to impress people! The house had seven bedrooms, a large garden, tennis court and field. My father planted fruit trees, and kept bees and chickens. Rolfe, an old chap helped him in the garden, he must have died in the early thirties.

Ultimately there were seven children in the family, Joan, myself (Peter), Eric, always known as Derry, Pam, Charlie, David and Brian who was the youngest by four years. The rest of us were very close together in age, one year between each. Mother had one live-in maid, sometimes two, but she often had trouble in keeping her servants. Poor old Edie was kept very busy but she was most capable and took it all in her stride! As we were a permanent household of eleven, meals were huge.

Father was tough; every morning he had a cold bath, he tried to get his children to take one, without success! He shaved with a cut-throat razor and cycled to work. The hours were long, the shop was open at 8.30a.m. and closed at 7p.m., 10p.m. on Saturdays; many deliveries were made by bicycle up to nearly midnight. Later these deliveries from the shop were made by an old 'Tin Lizzie', a model-T Ford.

Mr. Walter Longley and his five sons c.1926. Peter, the eldest, is on the left of his father.

The Downs Mill, Gunters Lane, a favourite place of the Longley children..

It is at 'West Leigh' that my earliest recollections are based. One of the first was being pushed down to the beach in a large pram over the footbridge at Collington Halt. There were no houses on the east side of Richmond Road; just a wide open space, which eventually became the Polegrove. At that time there were Canadian soldiers there on an assault course complete with hanging straw-filled sacks, which they charged with fixed bayonets! This must have been 1918.

In the early twenties a Miss Leale, the daughter of the vicar of St. Stephen's, came in the mornings to act as governess and teach my brother Derry and me our A.B.C. She also showed us how to milk a goat as the vicar kept them in the vicarage garden by the church. We also used to go further up the lane and watch Hoad's Mill grinding the flour. It was a very impressive sight close-to when it was working!

Our first school was a kindergarten in Amherst Road run by the Misses Sabin, two maiden ladies, who must have been very good teachers as we were soon reading quite fluently. In retrospect the thing that strikes me most about this period, as a contrast to-day, when my grandchildren mustn't cross the road without an adult and mustn't speak to strangers, is that I can never recollect ever having been taken to school.

My brother and I set out each morning, usually accompanied by Ted and Kenneth Eyles, the sons of the Devonshire Road jeweller, who also lived in Sutherland Avenue. We passed the Collington Mansions shops and the West Station, which was quite busy in those days. The West Station route was much quicker to London, some of the trains were through ones to Charing Cross or Cannon Street; when we went to London we always travelled on this line. There was a taxi-rank outside the station and one of the drivers, Fred, was courting my mother's maid, May. (They eventually married). That was an excuse to stop for a chat, but the big interest was the blacksmith's forge, just this side of Sackville Arch in Terminus Road. Its not altered much to-day, you can still see the chimney. There were nearly always horses being shod there and I can still smell the aroma of burning hooves as the still-hot horse shoes were nailed to them. So on through the Town Hall Square, past the Fire Station which was a distraction as we always looked at the engines, one of them was called 'Lady Kitty'. I still wonder how we ever got to school as the eldest of us was only seven years of age! Didn't have anyone to look after us with all our crowd but we never got into much trouble.

Our favourite playgrounds, apart from our large garden, were Collington Wood and the model yacht pond in Egerton Park, and during the summer our father would take us swimming at seven o'clock in the morning, either to the beach, (we had a beach-hut on the grass at the sea end of Richmond Road opposite the flagstaff), or, if the tide was out or the sea too rough, to the Egerton Park Baths.

Collington Pond, Bexhill.

Another favourite spot was the pond on the corner of Cranston Avenue (then only a gravel track) and Collington Lane. It was very good for tadpoles. This was just opposite the old Collington manor house, since demolished. There was a small stream which ran from the pond across the fields, under Collington Avenue and along in front of Collington Wood. It went under the railway by the Cattle Arch. I am not sure where it went then but it headed off in the direction of the Polegrove. The Cattle Arch was the predecessor of the Westcourt Drive railway bridge and was just a brick arch with a rough track and footpath through it. You will find that old Bexhillians (such as I) still refer to the Westcourt Drive bridge as the Cattle Arch and you may wonder what we are talking about.

At that time we could walk along the top of the open cliff from Richmond Road all the way to Cooden, and if tired (and had tuppence) we could travel back to Collington Halt along Cooden Drive on the open top deck of a tram.

Cooden Beach showing the trolly bus turning circle.

We could go from one end of the front to the other roller-skating, but had to avoid the Beach Inspector. I remember the Bath chairs which were pulled by men and hired; the old chaps didn't like it and thought we would collide with their waggons! The Colonnade area was the centre of activities, with the Rowing Club close and a band playing there. Where the De La Warr Pavilion stands was a row of coastguard cottages and the drinking fountain given by the son of the Maharajah of Cooch Behar in memory of his father. It had a metal cup on a chain which was rather unhygienic but we usually put our heads under the tap.

At the age of eight I went to Collington Rise School. The building is now flats at the bottom end of Collington Rise, and the school chapel, which was built while I was at the school, is in what is now Birkdale, though at that time it was part of the school playing fields.

The whole area from Sutherland Avenue to Little Common was then mainly schools and playing fields. Starting from the east there were Harewood and Normandale (boys), St. John's and Thornbank (girls), Mayfield (kindergarten), Collington Rise, St. Wilfreds, Lake House and

Seafield (boys) and Effingham House (girls). St. Wilfreds was burnt down about 1925 or 26 (much to our excitement and disappointment that it wasn't our school!). It was rebuilt later and renamed Falconbury.

There was much inter-school sporting rivalry and I can remember playing cricket at Harewood, Normandale, Lake House and Seafield. Sadly they are all gone now and the only original buildings still standing are Collington Rise and Lake House.

At the age of thirteen I won a scholarship to Mill Hill. All the family went to different schools. Derry and David went to University School, Hastings, Charlie won a scholarship to Dover College, while Joan and Pam went to Malvern Girls College. Brian followed Charlie to Dover College; by then the others had left school, these were the years of the depression and money was in short supply.

Bexhill in the 1920s was a very pleasant place in which to grow up, but being at boarding school I didn't see a lot of it. During the summer holidays the seafront was very busy with sandcastle competitions and donkey rides. The donkey man kept his animals in a small stable behind Longleys, it is now advertised as a desirable residence. I suppose we went to parties and that sort of thing but when one goes to boarding school one's friends are away. We were friends with Jo Eyles' two sons, Ken and Ted but we didn't get into the town a lot to meet people but knew some of them through our father who was a founder member of the Bexhill Rotary Club from 1923.

In 1927 or 28 father bought our first car, an old Austin 12, later he had an Armstrong Siddeley, as large as a tank, in order to fit in all the family he had a fender stool in the back facing the rear seats and the younger children sat on this!

There always appeared to be plenty going on in the town and West Bexhill was quite rural, whilst Little Common was a village on its own. There were three cinemas and a concert hall in the town, and in the Summer two concert parties, 'The Poppies' in Egerton Park and 'The Lawns' on what is now the De La Warr car park. In appearance the centre of the town and the seafront has changed little since those days but the surrounding area is hardly recognisable as the same place.

A double celebration took place in 1956 when Mr. and Mrs. Walter Longley celebrated their Golden Wedding which coincided with the 50th anniversary of the founding of Longley Bros. This picture shows members of the Longley family, from left to right back row, Joan, Martin Tiptaff (a director of the firm), Pamela, Peter and his wife Heather.

**Footnote:** *Peter Longley served in various theatres of war, he returned to Bexhill in 1946, but joined the Army Emergency reserve and was promoted to Lt. Colonel commanding 109 Transport Column RASC (AER). He retired from this branch in 1961 but became a member of the Regular Army Reserve of Officers in December of that year. Peter was Managing Director of Longley Brothers from 1946-1985 when the company was wound up. When Longley Bros. closed their store in Devonshire Road in 1984 headlines in the Bexhill Observer called it 'The End of an Era'. Peter has many interests, he was a JP and for some years Chairman of the Bench. He still lives in Cooden.*

# George Ransom born 1917

I was born in what they call the Brickyard Cottages, and there was say six little houses just where the infant school is, the new one of the two. Opposite Smith and Humphries, otherwise All Saint's Lane.

One could walk on the pavement, and see the people in the houses because the pavement was level with the windows. Turkey Road was only a stoney track with a pathway alongside it. The pathway was made by the men walking up to Turkey brickyard. And it gradually got wider and wider so a horse and cart could collect bricks, so my father tells me. Whitehouse Avenue was just a farm with a gate through to Downs Mill.

The new College was built in 1926. I had the pleasure of winning, as it was called then, a so-called scholarship. But my mum and dad couldn't afford to pay the £12 a quarter. And all the clothing you had to wear. Which was the red cap, properly dressed, with the six birds of the Sussex badge, grey stockings and then all the books. My mother couldn't do it.

George Ransom and his family lived in one of the cottages on the immediate left, situated in All Saints Lane, Sidley. c.1925.

George Ransom aged three.

I cheered. I did not want to leave my mates at St Peter's. That was in Chantry Lane then. Under Mr Bunting, the headmaster and Mr Davies, Mr Waite and Miss Withers were the teachers, it was an elementary school. In Mr. Bunting's class, I would like it to be known that in his class, you would have to sing hymns and pray all assembled (Mr. Ransom sang). 'Sit down, Standard Five.' Class, as you call them now, standards then. I also won a book, a prize for the best handwriting in the school that year, a year before I left Mr. Bunting's class. At school I used to clean the brass edge of the front door mat during my dinner time from school. You would have to do a long division sum and prove it to get out every night. Mr. Bunting, he would sit there doing his day's report or whatever and you got your sum, you went up to him, he would look at it. It was the finest training you can ever have, cause it learned you to concentrate your thoughts. I managed to please Mr. Bunting one day because I got a pass to play the piano at the London School of Music.

St. Peter's Boys, Mr. Waite's classes 1924.

When I started work, I worked for Mr Barnet the chemist. I suggested that on certain nights, Friday and Saturday, I delivered medicine on the bike. I can't quite remember what I was paid but I used to go to the golf club to work as a golf caddy. We used to earn 1/3d. and a three penny tip for cleaning clubs and do two rounds on a Saturday. I was quite happy really.

Some of my friends did quite well out of it. They went abroad with their respective golfers. I never got in to the depth of that. I was learning to play the piano. I also played the cornet in the town band at the Drill Hall on Thursday nights. The bandmaster, Mr Deeprose of Sidley, was a carpenter who worked for a local builder. One of the men, Councillor Berry, was very good to us. I played in the Bexhill Band from 14 (1931). I was also a member of the Bexhill Athletic Club. I used to run. Every month we had a monthly medal. Cecil Ballard who runs his business, as you know, greengrocery, was always the winner. I was always last. That was for a number of years. Reg Cane used to start us, well anyway he used to give me a start and everything. Never knew one side of my nose was blocked up; this affected my 5 to 6 mile race, thought it was my chest. 'Till I went into the army, never much good!

All Sidleyites had a gang. We used to play football for the school, watch Rooster Ransom play for Sidley. I was also a Boy Scout, 3rd. Bexhill. Our meeting place was behind the back of the now Working Men's Club. Sidley Boy Scouts was run by Mr. Livesey Dixon, a local solicitor.

My father worked for Stephen Carey, horse and cart. He went into the army, 1914 war. Then he worked for his uncle, S.G. Evans who had a brick yard , which is now Calgary Road and all that area. They used to fatten bullocks out in the fields; buy and sell, Dad used to run the whole thing, Kiteye Farm, do a coalround and wood, and coppice. Every bit of wood they chopped, they'd leave the wood to grow again, from that nothing was ever wasted. They would make faggots, bean poles, pergolas for gardens. As far as I can remember he earnt £1.19 shillings a week. Might have been £1.12 shillings. He was a manager of everything, a working manager, doing coal and everything. With this scholarship business it was hopeless. Dad and mum could not afford it as there were seven of us all at different schools, St. Barnabas, St. Marks (Little Common) and the Down. Mum took in washing from a Collington Lane school (Effingham House School) and that was delivered by the local pigman, G.S. Allen. Nice big basket of washing, 150 girls. I remember rows of washing. You'd sit down to your dinner and it would all drip down your neck! A boiler in the corner of the scullery. A brick job and you'd light a fire under it, that would boil the washing, see. Then there was a mangle. Everyone would have to turn that, even the postman. And there was always a Ludo championship going with a bottle of wine. Then the washing was carried down to the fields in Sidley brickyard. Mum hung the washing there. Adams used to make bricks, this house was built of the bricks (by my Dad, you know). One man would make 20,000 bricks, I think, say enough for one house every four weeks or something like that. Light a fire underneath them, and crowd them (first stacked and then burned). That's a thing in itself. In Dad's day one man used to do the 'pug light', about 20,000 bricks, Sidley Brickyard. Then they used to kill there. Kill animals, slit their throat, used to frighten me but I got used to it. Sling them up, wash them. Breed pigs. Then G.S. Allen moved in. The smell of the pig-wash! You didn't fancy eating it you know! Then there was a Mr. Zilwood, used to run a greengrocery business from there, he'd push a barrow.

The farm at Sidley Brickyard

Dad had a garden. Every plant he planted he would dip the root in a cow's pancake.

I've got a brother, yeh. He's retired now. He was a telegram boy during the war. A terrible job I expect, with delivering sad messages. He ended Head Postman.

Mum didn't make her own bread. There was a good baker in Sidley called Mr. Bert Arscott. He was responsible for the buying of Sidley Football ground. The shop used to be where now is the pet shop. There was a black cottage and a cobbler in a shed (Tom Bodle). We used to go down and get hot Hot Cross buns. Their bakery was in Beaconsfield Road, where they had another shop. But another Arscott was in St. Leonards Road, Bexhill; they were brothers, I think.

I always had a comic, *Comic Cuts* it was called.

Poaching. Oh yes, everybody had a catch of rabbits. I didn't, but if you went in the New Inn you could get one for 4d., eat it and then sell the skin for 2d. Regular fighting outside the New Inn on a Saturday night (properly refereed by somebody) generally over a woman, no kicking, code of honour. I played the piano every Saturday night at the New Inn for 4/6d. and a packet of fags.

Everytime there was an election we used to sing:

> Vote, vote ,vote for Mr. Courthope,
> Chuck old Ellis in the sea.
> If you wan't to vote you can,
> Mr. Courthope is your man,
> And we won't vote for Ellis any more.

We used to get paid 2d. for that. We celebrated Empire Day with red,white and blue rosettes, and sing 'Rule Britannia' and stand around the flag.

I first worked for Thatcher, the butcher in Belmont Terrace (next to the corner of Camperdown Street). Just for a few weeks. Mr. Thatcher was the local butcher. I earnt about 13 shillings a week.

When I was 13 or 14 (while I was still at school), I worked for Pocock at Old Town on a Saturday morning for 2/6d. Eight 'till one and walked with a basket all up and down Barrack Road and Dorset Road. And you always used to have to wear a white collar and tie just to deliver. It was heavy work. At the rear of that place they used to kill. I remember all the errand boys of Sidley. We would chase down to the beach with your old-fashioned costume at 10 o'clock at night, after work. Leave our bikes, they wouldn't get pinched.

Mert Thatcher, delivery boy for the Sussex Dairy, c.1926, on a bike similar to that used by George Ransom.

I then went to work at Messrs. Noakes & Co., Windsor Road, as an apprentice joiner. I never got round to the indenture business. I learnt the trade for 5 years, from 14 to 19. Then I went roofing on Larkins. Those days we done the roof, we done the 2nd fixing (windows, doors all that). A man named White actually cut the roof then we came along fixing. Those days I worked all down Walton Park. Every roof there. I am a carpenter/joiner. Then I started on Bexhill Corporation as carpenter. Then I joined the army at 23 for 5 years. After the war I went back to my old job.

Sidley Bugle Band celebrating the Coronation in 1937.

If you was ill there was no National Health you had to pay 2/6 or 7/6 to the doctor. Some used to say carry a nutmeg in your pocket against rheumatism. My grandmother in Chandler Road she worked until she was about 88 at Downs Laundry as a calender hand, and if you had been unwell she would give you port wine. The most popular doctor was Dr. Dick.

I first met my wife through the 'Imps' the Young Conservative Party. It was quite a main thing in Sidley on Thursday, our club night. And her club was at the Star Inn, Western Road, Bexhill, which is not there now. A big room at the back. We was Sidleyites and Miss Martin used to run that and we had a piano and a dance and that. That's how I met my wife.

We used to have dances at Sidley Institute to raise money for Bexhill Hospital. Messrs. Noakes (the company that I worked for) was involved in the joinery for the Hospital.

When I came out of my house the first thing I saw was a little tiny house where people named Cheeseman lived. He was the horse and cart driver of the Bexhill Corporation and the horse was based at the rear of the Town Hall and a blacksmith shop was there. And the Fire Brigade was there. Mr. Stevens the Captain. All volunteers. It was quite exciting when they all turned out. They'd fire the maroon. They were very smart. I remember once when they were testing a new fire engine and it ran away. The driver kept his wits and turned it up Station Road (now London Road) and stopped somewhere up by Russells Garage.

In Sidley there was a little wheelwright (Beal's) and Mr. Turner's house, the farrier (by Payless), and Mr. Catt the blacksmith.

The Lewes Lass was a ship broke up on the beach. I think it used to haul coal and timber. The Sidley brickyard buildings was built from timber off the pier (for coal) at bottom of Sea Road. My grandmother lived in a cottage in Sea Road, the only house there then.

Footnote: *George Ransom died before publication of this book. Members of his family still live in the town.*

## Ernest Claude Solomon born 1916

Ernest Claude Solomon was born in Cooden in 1916 where the booking office is now.

My father, he came from Ringmer and mother, she came from Buxted. He came just before the First World War and he was on the railway, a sub ganger, and I followed him in early 1936. I was on it right through the war up to I forget the exact date. I worked at the prison for a while, for a couple of years, but I got cheesed off with that because it was so demoralising, when I packed it up and went and worked at Liptons. That's where I finished my days. Little Common Lipton's, in 1982.

Our house was three up and two down, all that we had was a triangular shaped dining room and then a fairly big kitchen with a copper and all and sink up to the window, nice backyard and a lot of garden, it was a railway house actually.

The railway cottage at Cooden occupied by Ernest Solomon and his family.

There was a wooden halt, no station. There were a pair of semi detached, exactly the same, beyond the Cooden golf course. This is before 1936 when they started to demolish the houses and all and built the station.

Earl De La Warr designed it and he had poplar trees planted up Herbrand Walk to shield the station, but of course they don't grow down there and they all died. I remember when that was a rough old road, there was nothing where the hotel is.

A local train leaving Cooden Halt. c.1920.

What is the hotel now was all shops with living accommodation above. This end, that little place where they do hairdressing that was a photographer's, chap named Cheshire. Then he had the next bay window, the doorway is still there, that was a post office, all belonged to them. (There used to be a post box on the corner). You see a double fronted place, where the door was in the middle, that was Paines the greengrocer from Bexhill, colossal shop in the early 30s. Customers? There were big houses and monied people about Cooden in those days, but it didn't do anything so they closed down in the end. It was there for a quite a few years. Then there was a chap here, used to be in the village, he started up in the old coastguard cottages in Cooden. You know, opposite the hotel, they were in there. You've got that little low place, that was a garden to the next door neighbour when I lived at Cooden, 'cause that was railway ground, boundary stumps are still

The Cooden Beach Hotel.

there. If you go through the footpath they're by the end of that, to the back of these flats, then there used to be another little place there, it was still coastguards, something to do with the coastguards, little cottage, something like this house where I live now and it was a shop, then there was these two other little cottages which was knocked into one, Miss Arnold had it called Cove Cottage and turned it into kennels.

The coastguards cottages was knocked down and this side coming along towards the railway boundary fence was outhouses I suppose and that's where a chap from Little Common set up a greengrocery business, he did quite well, little old place. He did better than the chap from Bexhill.

I can remember quite a lot about Cooden. As you go from the hotel towards Bexhill, the first house on the right wasn't there, then there used to be a restaurant, they did teas, then there was nothing before you went round that bend to go down that little slope towards the Gatehouse what was. There was one big house up on the hill called 'The Bluff'. Nobody's got a photo of that but it was a marvellous old place, they knocked that all down to build all those silly new places they're building now. The Gatehouse was a marvellous hotel. Some big Swiss or Dutch firm bought it, they got away with murder, said it wasn't safe, well they're making money, they're building there now. Yet they haven't knocked down the two gate lodges.

One of my earliest memories is my mum and dad pushing me along Cooden Drive in the old wooden push chair with the spoke wheels and I can remember the army up on South Cliff. I can just remember that. Not Canadians, they had tents. Winceby House, that was all bare, nothing there at all. You come out of Beaulieu Road, there was a little copse there, nothing at all, on the left hand side hardly anything, along there. Trams ran along Cooden Drive.

My mum used to send me into Bexhill, she used to give me a penny to buy a couple of Chicago bars, like a dark toffee, beautiful they were. Used to have to catch the tram at the old Metropole where the De La Warr Pavilion is. I remember the hotel being pulled down. The old coastguard cottages that were there. There were two single rows of

Cooden Cliffs, Bexhill-on-Sea.

Church Hill Avenue, before the completion of the road. c.1925.

those cottages. Just two rows. I can't remember how many there were in each row. From the road to the sea they went, but they wasn't straight off the road. There were gardens and all there. Do you knows they couldn't knock them down with sledge hammers and nothing. They'd got huge thick walls and they had the fairground engineer, traction engine and put metal steel ropes all round to try and pull them down and it pulled the engine straight off the blocks. So in the end they had to have a crane there, with a big ball swinging to bash them down. No, the wire didn't cut them, it just pulled the engine straight off the jack, they blocked it up and they pulled it straight up like that. Had to knock them with the metal ball. There weren't coastguards living in them though, just people renting them.

We used to come up into Little Common. That shop at Pear Tree Lane, it was a general grocer's. Used to come up there shopping and all. He used to have big old bags on the floor, big old sacks, brooms, paraffin all the lot, even mice. But nobody was no worse off.

There was him and one along you know, it's an office now and newsagent before you come to Two Trees cafe, that's built on the old pond just after the war. Right opposite was a row of shops. The Post Office and Saunders the grocers, there wasn't another one till you come to Tim's the ironmongers.

Old Charlie Duke, he was a character, we used to go along there and get arrowroot biscuits and all in waxed paper bags at dinner time for school cause we never went back to Cooden for dinner. We used to go along there. Happy days!

In 1930 when I was 16 the pond was still there, it wasn't filled in before the war. There wasn't the big houses like there is today. Opposite my house here in Church Hill, Little Common Road where we've lived since 1942 wasn't a road, it was all open ground, people next door used to hang their washing out there and have goats down there. All that was a rough old track, there was nothing down there that side of the road, the south side. The council houses wasn't there. Coal cart used to come up there and tip the coal out of the vans, it was only a tip cart, tip coal out with the blessed great pot holes. There were holly trees we used to get in and play, there used to be a pond there where the council houses are built now in Shepherds Close.

My father worked on the railway till he retired. He was a ganger on the track, same as me. My mum she was one of 21. No television in those days! My mother was 90 something when she died. Yes, I have plenty of cousins. My mother lived at Cooden and then she went to Eastbourne 'cause they had to get out of the house, they put her in one at Eastbourne. She died at my sister's place in Hailsham. I've also got a brother at Scunthorpe.

St. Mark's Church, and on the left of this the village school.

I was at school at St Marks up the hill where the car park is now. If you look up the other side of the Institute in the car park, along the church wall, the wall is still white, the one nearest the wall was the girls' toilet and the one half way down was the boys' toilet. The white is still on the wall.

We had long wooden seats at school. Mr Card the headmaster was strict, you ain't kidding. My mate used to sit and make faces and I burst out laughing. 'Come out Solomon, hold out your hand', and he had a cane which he brought across my hand. Oh dear, oh dear. I couldn't hold a pen or nothing. Another time I called out to a teacher after school, called Ella, her name was Ella. I said, 'Good night Ella'. She told Tommy Card and next day at playtime he asked me to stay back. He said, 'I'm going to cane you for calling after my teacher after school'. I said, 'It's nothing to do with you what I do after school, I'm not on the school ground'. 'Oh yes it is,' he said, 'hold out your hand.' I struggled and struggled and he picked me up by my trousers and he split them right up the back side. He was a first aid man so he got out the first aid and he sewed them up with safety pins. 'You can't sit down now,' he said, 'so you can go out and clean the gardening tools'.

We used to have allotments then where Alexander Court is now. Just up the back, lovely allotments, we used to grow our own vegetables and go over to Lake House or do them for a flower show exhibit of our stuff. Mr Card used to get me to push the wheel barrow along there, he'd give you a good hiding one minute and a bit of currant duff the next day, on a plate with sugar all on it. His wife just stayed in the house, she wasn't a teacher. He's been dead now several years but his daughter, Barbara Card, lived in Potman's Lane but recently she's moved to a flat in Wickham Avenue.

Gardening at school was only for the boys, the girls did needlework or stool ball. Allotments belonged to the church. About a dozen. You had your own little patch, and you had to double trench it every year. Take a spit out and take it down the bottom, and leave a trench, turn top in and other on the top of that so it got really turned over like a bed would be.

I walked to school, sometimes, if it rained, we caught the bus ld return. You had to get out climbing up the hill and help push the old thing, little Ford bus with roller blinds up the side. Dan Thomas was the driver.

I think we lived better in those days than we did now. Because we'd probably have a steak and kidney pudding, a big pudding mid-week. Something else and perhaps a small roast, Sunday we had meat. All cooked on an old kitchen range. My dad grew his vegetables, made it quite interesting.

The Gardening Group of boys from St. Marks School in 1929, with their headmaster Mr. Card. Amongst those who can be identified are Deeprose, Cheese, Green, Hemmings, Antick, Catt and Pennells. Holding the wheelbarrow is Ernest Solomon.

I didn't go on the beach a lot, I used to come up the village with my mates. Play up here with my mates. Could play in the road then. I never forgot when I came down the hill with my old hoop, it went adrift, and the verger in those days was an ex-marine sergeant major and he always went into the Wheatsheaf and I was running after my hoop and he came down the hill on his bike and went up my backside with his front wheel, and the language! I think my hoop nearly melted and the road caught fire. Dear oh dear. He used to be the same when he went in the Wheatsheaf. I don't think he had much brakes on his bike but surely he could have seen me.

Cooden Sea Road, originally Camp Road, along which Ernest Solomon walked to school.

In my teens I went courting anywhere. We used to go to Bexhill a lot cause there was a fun fair along the front by the old Pavilion (not the De La Warr). On that bit of ground there used to be a fun fair, scooters, cars, fruit machines. The old bus office was opposite. There used to be a shelter, we called it the Monkey Shelter (it was neither round nor square), but it used to be near there where the old Pavilion was, but it's all gone now.

Cooden Sea Road

Little Common Village

Right along the front there used to be all green. Bushes along by the road, there were seats in there you could sit out of the wind. But it's all gone. Like an evergreen hedge, laurel, east side of the Pavilion, going right along the front, The promenade was broken off to the road by these little places, but that only went as far as the Sackville, I think it did, a lawn and a little border round, and these seats, but it's all tarmac now . It's the same as you come down Devonshire Road to go across the road by the club. You go straight down Channel View, well on that very corner, what's the car park now, there used to be a colossal building Marine Mansions, Findlaters on the corner facing east used to be a big wine merchant. There was another shop there sold materials. Colossal buildings. The old Metropole, that was something. I used to go to the Metropole to have a drink because the Star Brewery used to be there, lovely stuff that was, 4d a pint. It was a place you went for a drink, and a hotel where people came and stayed like. It had a fire and then it got damaged, then they pulled it down because of the De La Warr. It was a lovely building went that way, sort of sideways to the sea. We don't go to the De La Warr much now, we're cut off in Little Common, no bus after 5.20 pm. I remember the Poppys (entertainers). I never went, I remember them in Egerton Park. I didn't go away much but I used to stay with my grannie, my dad's mother, at Ringmer. They had a farm and I used to wear the old fashioned plimsolls, my feet got soft walking up through the stubble. That's where I went for my summer holidays. I don't think my parents went away. In those days there wasn't much money to save to go away was there? My father didn't go out much, he worked in his garden.

I learnt to drive when I was about 11, when Barnhorn Lane (sic) was being built. It was when Sainsbury's first came to Bexhill down the bottom of Devonshire Road. Men had peaked caps, striped aprons, tucked up in the corner, black gaiters. The man who taught me to drive worked for them, he used to deliver goods to our house. One day he said, 'Solly you've been watching me driving, now it's your turn'. I've been driving ever since. I just watched him and never crashed the gears or nothing. I left school at 14, then got job at a garage and did odd jobs, taxi work, etc. Lots of people used taxis; take people out to have tea at

Ernest Solomon, the eldest son with his parents, Alice and Ernest (snr.), Gwen and Cyril.

Herstmonceux and back home. I was a taxi driver before I started on the railway, getting 25/- a week driving the 24hp Sunbeam saloon. I left because there was a bit more money on the railway.

When I started on the railway I got 44/- a week in 1936, 48/- actually cause 4/- was danger money for working beside a live rail. 48 hours, 1/- an hour. What would they pay you to do the job like that now? My mum took some of it, but she saved quite a bit up, she didn't tell me but when I got married, she'd got quite a bit put by.

I worked on the track. Seven of us then, then it ended up with 6, then 4. I was ganger in the latter days, and I ended up with nobody. I was on my own and they were getting ready for this mobilisation. Now instead of 7 men to look after 5 miles of track, that's 2 and three quarter miles each way, from Cooden to near Norman's Bay, there's only 4 looks after the track between Lewes to Glynde Gap and they run about in a van all day long. You see the yellow van with the blokes sitting in it, and those German mechanical machines that go round doing the job.

We had levels, that was the maintenance. And weeds, getting rid of weeds up the side, mowing the embankments with a scythe, I'd like to see chaps trying to do that now, with scythes. I've worked from this end of Beaulieu road to one quarter mile the other side of Rockhouse Bank, the house other side of Norman's Bay on the top of the hill, that farmhouse has gone now. Quarter mile the other side of that, 7, then to a gang of 4 then nobody, so there we are. They were all steam trains I worked on up till later part of '36 the electric started when I went on but it wasn't fully operative then because they had a lot of trouble. They used to have to take the engine off and bring the motor train, push and pull.

When I left school I belonged to a little club in St Marks Close. Kind of man's club, you only paid a tanner a week or something, play billiards darts, dances, bonfire and things in the Institute too. Those were good days they were. Used to have fun. It's still called the Institute now and right opposite there was a garage, where the school buses came from, and we used to sit on the steps of the Institute and watch them cleaning them and filling them with petrol. It was a sort of village hall. Just had it re-roofed and refurbished inside. I know 'cause my grand daughter had her wedding reception there.

I didn't play football, but I used to play golf. Along at Cooden. Remember especially old Major Lawrence, he was an ex sergeant major, he was a good old chap. We'd come home from school and he'd come over the garden fence and proper sergeant major shouting, 'Solomon, would you come and caddy for us or for so and so.' I used to go out and earn about half a crown, I used to go up there before I left school, and remember the girls caddying. They used to wear rompers and lace up boots.

In those days Fred Robinson used to be there and his son used to make all the golf clubs in the shop, only wooden ones. Used to come in a block and they used to have to shave them all off and they used to have News of the World Tournaments there years ago. Big matches, but that's all gone. I like Highwoods, but I prefer Cooden. I taught myself to play. I used to get on the sand with a couple of old balls, cause they go well along dry sand. I used to play with the others, but never did anything. I don't play now cause my arm's all messed up and can't swing a club properly.

Bexhill has changed. I think now they are on about a car park, that they should park echelon fashion down Devonshire Road. It was all trees and had these island up the middle of the road, with these double lamps on. The trams went on either side. Trams used to come down Devonshire Road, along by the De La Warr and down Egerton Road, Brockley Road and along Cooden Drive. Then when the trolley buses took over, they went up Western Road then, as well as going down Brockley Road and up the other way.

If they have car parking over the station or Sainsburys it will see Warburtons go, very old firm, they had to get out of Belle Hill. Used to keep the station horses by Town Hall Square and in the square itself there used to be a tank, an old first war tank, then it got shifted to Egerton Park, I think it was. It was on the side where the shops are, I don't know where it came from.

Horses used to do the deliveries, for the railway, during the war, yes. Horses were stabled at where Sainsburys is now, where the shops start going down to Town Hall Square. The entrance to the car park is where you went into the goods yard, then the toilets and then there used to be market stalls, as far as the corner, some stalls under the arch, with the old hurricane lamps and all. Salvation Army used to play in that little triangle by Windsor Road. Outside the Town Hall they played on Saturdays. I was down Bexhill more often than not then.

Regarding society in Bexhill, to be quite truthful with you they were snobs. That is the word, they were monied people. But I find during the war that everyone was Tom, Dick and Harry. Now if it takes a war to bring you all together it doesn't make sense to me. It's the same along the Legion Club. There used to be a bloke come in and he'd say, 'I'm Major'. I said , 'You're not a major, you're Tom or Bill'. I said, 'When you are out of the army that's finished'. I said, 'You could call me Ganger'. 'Cause I was a ganger on the railway, 'I've finished work so that's it'. That to me was snobbish. I hate people coming up to me and saying, 'Good afternoon Solomon'. That gets up my goat. I can't stick it. There's one or two around this village and I just walk away. To me it's horrible. I've always been brought up to say 'Mister' or 'Sir'. But I've got a handle to my name same as you or anybody else. I don't mind a nickname but not just my surname.

There were quite a lot of retired people coming into the town before the war. You'd be surprised. There was all the old majors and colonels coming to Bexhill, come to die and they forgot what they came for. It's been like it ever since.

When you went to Bexhill you daren't whistle, they'd be looking out of the window and perhaps the bobby'd come along, 'cause you were whistling or singing. Majority of people aren't so snobbish now. Round here they call me Solly and I call them Doris or whatever they like to be called.

I was an errand boy. There was a grocers shop down the bottom of Western Road near the library. I used to go out in the morning with the carrier bike and order book and collect orders and go back, put them up, and go out with the van and deliver them in the afternoon. That was in the early 30s. Then I was errand boy up another shop, place just this side of the Classic Cinema, I still call it the Playhouse, farm and produce shop. I used to take the van out sometimes or go on a bike if it was just a little way. One Christmas the old grocer, I used to have to scrub the floor on my hands and knees, it was past 11 at night cause we'd had a lot of orders to take out and do you know what that old devil said to me? 'Oh! Mrs So and So in Peartree Lane wants a quarter of ham can you take it out'. I wasn't happy about that but I took it. I didn't get nothing extra. Can you imagine a boy doing it today?

To be quite truthful, I think the younger generation are damned lazy, cause it doesn't matter what you mention you can adapt yourself to do anything. Now the last days; I was behind the provision counter at Lipton's, I was doing bacon and all, I was only shown, never touched the side of bacon before. I knew all the cuts. You've only got to use your brain. But it's too easy on the dole, too easy. We never drawn the dole. We never been out of work, one day on strike on the railway, cause I had to, just one day, got 2/6d.

Bexhill has changed quite a lot as a seaside town I think. You don't get the people here like you used to. The beach used to be packed along Bexhill front. More than what you get now. They used to have the band along the Colonnade, there used to be a bandstand and then it got wrecked by the sea years ago and we used to go along and listen to them of a Sunday evening.

It's all changed now. You don't see the old dears in the old wicker chairs holding the handle, steering it with the wheel in front with a handle. Being pushed along the sea front or steering themselves.

Horses and carriages and lots of blacksmiths. You know the antique shop, opposite the Wheatsheaf. That used to be blacksmith. Man there made a hoop for a ha'penny, an iron hoop. It used to be lovely there and then he went to where the garage is, Crockers. He closed before the war, that garage was before the war. The roundabout wasn't always there. It was just a crossroads. Just green by the crossroads. I remember when the old chap was dying in the Wheatsheaf and they put straw on the road to stop making a clatter. He had to pay for it, used to be deep on the road, if you were seriously ill. You had to get permission. It was there till he passed away.

Then the pub wall this end, just in Barnhorn Lane (sic) there used to be a big case outside with all the cups, football, cricket and all. Can you imagine that on the wall today? In a case outside the Wheatsheaf on the wall. A glass case, under the window. Can you imagine it staying there today?

Lots less crime then. Mother used to walk up from Cooden up here to the village shop and left the back door and front door open, windows and all. Go back home, no trouble. We lock now. I expect our back door is locked now. Now if anyone comes to the front door I peep out of the curtains, if anybody knocks and if I don't know them I don't answer.

Footnote : *During the war Ernest Claude Solomon was in a reserved occupation. 'That annoyed me, but I was in the Home Guard on the railway and we had the King's uniform and all exactly the same as a Tommy. We were stationed in a school at Bulverhythe and took the train down there to St. Leonards.' The British Legion now recognise the Home Guard.*